TEACHING
CIVIC LITERACY
PROJECTS

TEACHING CIVIC LITERACY PROJECTS

STUDENT ENGAGEMENT WITH SOCIAL PROBLEMS
Grades 4–12

Shira Eve Epstein

Foreword by Celia Oyler

Teachers College
Columbia University
New York and London

Published by Teachers College Press, 1234 Amsterdam Avenue, New York, NY
10027

Copyright © 2014 by Teachers College, Columbia University

Library of Congress Cataloging-in-Publication Data is available at www.loc.gov

ISBN 978-0-8077-5575-4 (paper)
ISBN 978-0-8077-7332-1 (ebook)

Printed on acid-free paper
Manufactured in the United States of America

21 20 19 18 17 16 15 14   8 7 6 5 4 3 2 1

Contents

Foreword

The weekend before I sat down to read Shira Eve Epstein's wonderful book, *Teaching Civic Literacy Projects: Student Engagement with Social Problems, Grades 4–12*, I attended a family mindfulness and nature retreat. On Saturday morning all of the adults and children engaged in a walking meditation along the shore of Lake Norwich. At one point we stopped walking and selected perches on large rocks, where we sat in silence, giving us an opportunity to observe the glistening ripples on the surface of the lake. On Monday morning, when I began to read Shira's book, which invites teachers to design classroom civic literacy projects, the image of the lake with its unseen undercurrents and endless ripples kept returning to my mind's eye.

As teachers we offer our students opportunities to learn about the world, yet we can never fully know all the effects of our work—exactly what students take with them and then how that knowledge ripples outward. Yes, we have formative and summative assessments that give us various degrees of information about what our students are learning, what skills they have mastered, what content knowledge they have amassed, or what concepts they have learned, but what do students take with them and apply in the world beyond school? How does the learning students engage with in school inform their knowledge of themselves, their identities, and their commitments to their families and communities? What aspects of school learning prepare graduates to navigate independently and interdependently in the world and successfully negotiate adult life? And finally, when does school curriculum help prepare youth to be active *shapers* of the world's future? For as Shira explains in Chapter 1, "Teachers who enact civic literacy projects position students as agents, not passive recipients of knowledge. . . . Civic literacy projects ask students to critically reflect on their lives and society at large and then act on their reflections" (p. 11). As they act on these reflections, what are the ripple effects for our world? This book invites us to engage students in the serious work of civic uplift as part of school: Why wait until adulthood to get involved in making the world a better place?

As a teacher with a life-long commitment to school curriculum, that, as Shira puts it, helps "students find a place for themselves in civic life" (p. 33), I was deeply inspired by the teachers and students profiled here who do not sit idly by and feel overwhelmed or apathetic about local and global social issues. Instead, there are numerous, varied, and rich descriptions in these pages of teachers inviting young people to take up complex problems such as environmental racism, segregation, and teenage sexual health.

Situating these teachers' work within the long and noble tradition of curriculum for social change, Shira reminds us that, unfortunately, public schools are traditionally places to teach obedience and civics is very often taught "with a form of academic detachment" (p. 30). Community engagement and community improvement are not typically in the standards or on the standardized tests that purport to measure student learning or teacher effectiveness. Nevertheless, Shira demonstrates through the detailed descriptions of the teachers who so generously shared their practices, that civic literacy projects can indeed be conducted in our current climate when top-down mandates sometimes threaten to become the only curriculum.

Shira set out to carefully document teachers' practices and, from years of learning from teachers, she teases out a simple and elegant three-part frame for designing civic literacy projects: Naming, Knowing, Acting. First, students go through a process to name injustices in the world; then, using a "plurality of viewpoints (p. 5)," they employ a wide variety of multimodal tools and genres to dig deeply into the issues; finally, using a range of literacy practices, they take action to try to influence others through such media as filmmaking, speeches and presentations, poetry and narrative writing, persuasive and investigative writing, murals, workshops, and lobbying.

Reading these civic literacy projects helps me imagine a national education policy that challenges schools to dive into the project of teaching for democracy and pluralism and to work to achieve "liberty and justice for all." Shira's work offers us a reflection of democratic practice in the classroom, through the teaching of critical reading, persuasive writing, and deliberation. To help students appreciate the ever-changing undercurrents of pluralism we must teach them to develop their own analyses of issues and to struggle assiduously to understand multiple other perspectives. The ripple effect of these important pedagogical efforts encourages students to engage in the never-ending project of working towards a more just society. In *Teaching Civic Literacy Projects: Student Engagement with Social Problems, Grades 4–12*, Shira invites us all to contemplate the depth of the democratic project and the possibility that schools can help uphold our democratic ideals.

—Celia Oyler

Preface

In the months following September 11, 2001, as a middle school English language arts teacher in the Bronx, New York City, I stumbled on the idea that my students could write letters to the mayor proposing their ideas about what should be built at the World Trade Center site. It was with this relatively underdeveloped assignment that my curiosity about civic education began. Questions about how feet-on-the-ground educators support youth to read, write, and speak about relevant, civic issues have driven multiple projects I have since pursued with youth of varying ages. Through these exposures, I have learned how students can have a say about social problems in the real world beyond the four walls of a classroom. In this book, I share what I have learned about how to support this type of youth civic participation.

This preface further elaborates on the book's intended purpose, provides a chapter-by-chapter overview, and identifies my assumed primary audience. It concludes with an acknowledgement of those who guided me as I wrote this book.

PURPOSE

Teaching Civic Literacy Projects: Student Engagement with Social Problems, Grades 4–12 illustrates for teachers how to enact robust forms of civic education in today's schools. Its purpose is to be instructive and thought-provoking, inspiring teachers to craft curriculum addressing civic topics such as immigration policy reform, environmental damage, and gun control. To this end, I separate civic projects into three key components—problem identification, problem exploration, and action—and provide authentic examples from classrooms when analyzing each component. Problem identification involves selecting the social problems that will be addressed through the projects. Here, students name pressing needs and injustices in society through methods such as journal writing and discussion, and they ultimately choose one, or a set of problems, as their focus. Problem exploration entails students' studying their selected problem to reveal its complexity.

This involves consulting multiple resources including newspaper articles and films to better understand how people experience the problem and what possible solutions are available. Finally, when students take action, they advocate for change and the amelioration of their identified problem by presenting crafted messages to particular audiences. During this phase, students write letters, produce digital videos, and organize meetings—just to name some possibilities—to make change.

This work has much value. First, sustained civic projects on relevant social problems can motivate youth to get involved in their schoolwork (Bomer, 2004) and create opportunities for students to develop skills needed for community participation and social critique (Westheimer & Kahne, 2004). All the while, they ask students to read, write, and speak, developing their literacy skills. For this reason, the projects are identified as civic literacy projects in this book. On a broader scale, the projects ask students to play a part in ensuring a strong democracy where they serve "a public good that is also their own" (Barber, 1992, p. 256) and take civic action that is informed and engaged (Parker, 2003). *Teaching Civic Literacy Projects: Student Engagement with Social Problems, Grades 4–12* presents and analyzes pedagogy to this end.

OVERVIEW

The arc of the book moves from the general to the specific. In Chapter 1, I speak about civic engagement broadly, introducing key motivating principles that teachers draw on when enacting civic projects. In the next three chapters, I talk more concretely about how teachers support each component of a project—problem identification (Chapter 2), problem exploration (Chapter 3), and action (Chapter 4). I offer pedagogical ideas that can be readily used in classrooms. In Chapter 5, I tease out critical tensions that play out during all three phases. These tensions are related to how civic literacy projects can foster both student independence and collaboration, ask youth to work in solidarity with others and advocate for their own shared needs, and require students to engage with controversial issues.

In Chapter 6, I outline a curriculum design process for teachers to use to ensure coherent and meaningful projects driven by clear goals and instruction that is aligned with the goals. Chapter 6 also presents a number of practical tools (i.e., templates, worksheets) that could be modified for immediate teacher and student use during civic literacy projects. Preservice teachers, first learning the art of curriculum design, are likely to particularly appreciate this chapter as it outlines a step-by-step process for planning and enacting civic literacy projects.

TARGET AUDIENCE

The text is written for preservice classroom teachers, inservice classroom teachers, and youth educators working in out-of-school settings who wish to enact civic projects with youth. I offer examples of educators working with upper-elementary, middle school, and high school students. Readers working with youth in any of these age groups will be able to find advice on how to enact civic literacy projects with them. For teachers working in or preparing to teach in schools, I discuss how civic literacy projects can be enacted in English and social studies classes, as well as classes that are not linked to any one content area but are generally focused on improving students' academic achievement and leadership skills (e.g., advisory classes). Therefore, educators involved in these parts of the school curriculum will be particularly aided. Other potential audiences include school administrators interested in supporting youth civic engagement projects and teacher educators looking to teach preservice teachers how to enact socially oriented projects.

All potential audiences will find in this a book a portrayal of youth civic engagement projects as do-able yet never simple. I break civic literacy projects into manageable parts while illustrating their variations and the thought-provoking tensions that run through them.

ACKNOWLEDGMENTS

I thank the brave, creative, and welcoming teachers and students portrayed in this book. They have allowed me to spend months with them, asking unending lists of questions in order to understand youth civic engagement. The names of these individuals, as well as the names of their schools and organizations, are replaced by pseudonyms within the body of the book to protect their anonymity. Given this research guideline, I cannot thank them by their real names, but my gratitude is real and deep.

I thank my mentors who have helped me develop the key ideas that undergird this book. Two deserve particular attention. Celia Oyler has offered years of critical feedback that has been the primary informant of my development as a teacher educator, researcher, and writer. Peter Levine has introduced me to organizations, individuals, and ideas that have meaningfully shaped my research agenda and writing.

I thank all the people who have read drafts of this book. My writing group—David Allen, Elisabeth Johnson, Melissa Schieble Pirro, and Jason Wirtz—read outlines and chapter drafts, always offering new ideas to push me forward. Jessica Lipschultz also gave her amazingly productive attention to the entire book. To these editors and all other friends and colleagues who have informed my thinking about this book—your work is priceless.

I thank the Kettering Foundation, located in Dayton, Ohio. In attending Foundation meetings, my conceptions of democracy and deliberation grow. I am also grateful that the Foundation saw the potential of my study of the park project (one of the anchor cases reviewed in the book). The original study of the park project, in which I analyzed the teachers' and students' experiences, was conducted in association with the Foundation, and it was all the better because of this collaboration. Specifically, Libby Kingseed provided editing that enabled my message in this book, and in other pieces, to clearly emerge.

I thank Jews for Racial and Economic Justice (JFREJ), a membership-based organization in New York City. As an active member for over 10 years, I have learned firsthand from this community the promise and complexity of community organizing. I leave each meeting asking myself how educators and youth can develop the skills that JFREJ members use to make social change. Additionally, the brilliant and kind executive director, Marjorie Dove Kent, lent her valuable time to discuss some of the issues covered in this book.

I thank everyone at Teachers College Press who made this book a reality. I especially thank Marie Ellen Larcada and Karl Nyberg, who were forever caring and clear about what to do next.

I thank my beloved family. My mother and father, Shirley and Norman Epstein, two career teachers, showed nonstop enthusiasm and interest in my progress, always asking about the book with excitement. My mom is the ultimate cheerleader who helps me feel that I can take on any project, including this book. My dad provides a steady political and ethical compass, enabling me to name and analyze both the social troubles *and* the social wonders in this world. I hear his voice in my head as I think about ways to advocate for a common good.

David, you have watched me write this book most closely. Over the years, you have brilliantly assumed so many different roles to help me through. You were an editor, pouring over drafted pages and proposing important recommendations. You readily entertained hours of conversation, allowing me to work through ideas with your helpful insight. And you supported this process by managing many details of our life together—including the caring of our wonderful son, Yadin!—ensuring that I had the time and mental space to finish this book. You are my partner, through and through.

CHAPTER 1

Civic Literacy

In the closing months of the school year, the 7th-graders in Class 306 were practicing the skills of civic engagement, studying a problem affecting their community and organizing a collective response. Their 7-week project began when two students informed Deanne Holly, the English and social studies teacher, and Lucy Oaks, the collaborating special education teacher, that state budget cuts threatened the funding of a beloved, local park. Located in an urban low-income community predominated by residents of color, the park provided a valuable space for the students to spend their summer vacations. Without adequate funding, the park's hours would be shortened and the outdoor pool would stay closed. This alone could have rallied the community, yet there was another reason for concern. The park had been created as a negotiated concession for the neighborhood's burden of housing a water sewage plant that emitted noxious fumes. The placement of the plant was contentious as it was originally proposed to be located in a higher-income community with fewer residents of color. Years of advocacy had brought about the park as a compromise, and the looming budget cuts challenged this arrangement.

The students and teachers were motivated to address the problem through the curriculum. The previous year, they had studied a nearby university's expansion into their neighborhood and how it would affect the buildings and streets with which they had grown up. The project had been organized with the help of a nonprofit community-based organization, which provided a staff member to visit the students weekly and guide their studies of the university expansion. This year, the teachers planned to take more responsibility for the students' civic work and embed a civic project into the content areas, excited to try out a type of teaching that was relatively new to them. Deanne and Lucy responded to the 7th-graders' enthusiasm about the park budget and suggested that they focus on it in class.

Following weeks of research on the budget cuts, the students sent letters to their local assemblyperson expressing their concern about the cuts and offering potential solutions—work that ignited the students' sense of purpose and self-worth. One made this comment:

As a result of this project, I feel proud of myself. And not only me, but of all the people that tried to make something to help it. . . . We didn't only do it for us but we did it for thousands of people that went to the park.

This student is aware of her potential to use her voice in her community, and she recognizes the power of working with and for others. Another student articulated a commitment to involving others in their cause: "I absorbed all this information, and now I go around and I'm telling people what happened and they're passing it on. And more people are being aware of it and they're wanting to do more about it." Here we see glimpses of youth as engaged civic actors.

I have had the privilege of learning from various educators and youth, including those in Class 306, who address public issues through sustained projects. I have watched and at times guided such projects in urban schools with students in late elementary grades through early high school. Most of my learning has been with poor and working-class students of color. I have also had opportunities to work with White students of privilege. I have seen the English and social studies content areas be used as sites for civic engagement and have also seen these projects unfold in advisory periods and after-school programs. Despite these differences, all the teachers and students I have met through my research on civic education have helped me understand how youth can be supported to name and analyze social problems around them and take action, working for a better world. Classes I have met enacted the following projects:

- **The social justice writing assignment**—Guided by their English and social studies teacher, students in an 8th-grade class created varied texts (i.e., posters, PowerPoint presentations, letters) on multiple problems of social concern. These problems included the poor nutritional value of fast food, the pressures of standardized testing, and the AIDS epidemic in Africa. The year concluded with an assembly in which students shared their messages with their classmates.
- **The safe sex health project**—This project entailed 9th-graders, two advisory teachers, and youth workers from a nonprofit organization called Urban Youth planning and running a day-long, grade-wide safe sex health fair. Feeling uninformed about how to make good decisions about their sexual health, the students set out to design a youth-oriented fair that they felt would give themselves and their peers needed information in this area.
- **The race awareness after-school program**—With the support of a nonprofit organization, Beyond Today, 4th- and 5th-grade students

from de facto segregated schools came together for multiple out-of-school meetings to build friendships and an awareness of race and racism in society. At the conclusion of the year, they created a video public service announcement on school inequity and other issues related to de facto segregation.

- **The park project**—As introduced above, this project involved 7th-grade students protesting budget cuts to a local park. Through their English and social studies classes, the class conducted research on the state budget and the proposed cuts and wrote letters to their local assemblyperson persuading him to restore the park's budget.

These four cases serve as the anchor cases for this book. I used qualitative methods, including classroom observations and teacher and student interviews, to study them, and I now draw on them to describe a process for teachers to consider as they enact civic literacy projects. I also reference related literature portraying other groups of youth, from elementary, middle, and high school grades, studying and acting to improve society.

Specifically, I have learned from these educators and youth how civic projects entail three key phases (see Figure 1.1). Phase 1 involves identifying

Figure 1.1. Phases of Civic Literacy Projects

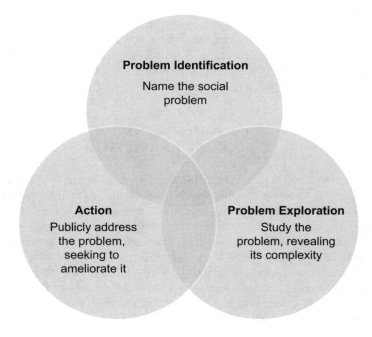

Problem Identification

Name the social
problem

Action

Publicly address
the problem,
seeking to
ameliorate it

Problem Exploration

Study the
problem, revealing
its complexity

civic problems, Phase 2 involves the study and exploration of these problems, and Phase 3 involves designing and taking action steps to address
them. These phases incorporate essential civic literacy skills including naming and critiquing forms of bias and systemic inequities, reading widely and
critically, responding to social issues in ways that are sensitive to complexities of problem-solving and to the multiple people involved, and acting with
agency (Robinson, 1998). Given their importance, I review each phase in
the subsequent chapters.

As I illustrate the varying ways these phases can unfold in a civic literacy project, I align myself with scholars who prioritize a study of teaching
processes, not exclusively the results of these processes. While we want to
form a reasonable idea of how students respond to particular pedagogical
approaches, educators, administrators, and researchers too often focus dis-
proportionately on results and not the teaching that leads to the results. In
turn, they pursue "the search for a scientific basis for teaching" and aim to
identify "generic teacher behaviors and strategies associated with student
achievement" (Feiman-Nemser, 1990, p. 223). I find this search for generic
practices shortsighted. Such a technical orientation suggests that there is a
uniformly correct way of teaching for all students and glosses over teachers' contextualized decisionmaking. Countering an exclusive reliance on this
approach, others adopt a practical orientation and emphasize "elements of
craft, technique, and artistry that skillful practitioners reveal in their work,"
as well as the way that "teachers deal with unique situations" (Feiman-
Nemser, 1990, p. 222). I favor this practical approach that acknowledges
the uncertain job of teaching and the different ways that teachers and students pursue excellence. Therefore, in this book I highlight variations of
effective teaching and provide several options for teachers to consider when
enacting civic literacy projects.

KEY COMPONENTS OF
CIVIC LITERACY PROJECTS

To foreshadow what will be more fully explored in the coming chapters,
here I briefly review what is involved in problem identification, problem
exploration, and action. In problem identification, students name concerns
they have about their society, often citing those impacting their personal
lives. In this phase, students raise questions such as: "Why do so many of
my friends have asthma?" "Why is my country at war?" "Why is there
malnutrition in developing countries?" "Why are the LGBTQ [lesbian, gay,
bisexual, transgender, queer/questioning] youth in my school bullied?" Or,
instead of raising questions, at first students can list all the problems of
which they are aware, such as "war" or "bullying." In this process, students

put on critical lenses and share what worries them about their community and society.

During problem exploration, students work with print and nonprint texts that help them answer their questions or understand the problems they named. For example, in the types of civic engagement projects discussed in this book, students do not say, "Homelessness is a problem" and then move straight to an action step such as collecting used clothing to give to a shelter. In order to better understand the dilemma of homelessness, imagine a class interviewing homeless citizens or community organizers working on this issue, reading policy statements on how governmental bodies aim to address homelessness, and watching a movie portraying the struggles of a homeless family. Students may also be invited to speak about their own experiences as homeless youth or aiding homeless neighbors. In these steps, students are introduced to multiple factors that impact the experiences of homeless individuals. During problem exploration, teachers and students engage with a plurality of viewpoints and experiences with any one civic problem.

In the third phase, action, students take steps to address and potentially ameliorate the problem. If they choose to write persuasive letters to government officials or launch websites that bring attention to their issue, they are taking action by creating texts, using their "pens as agents" (Robinson, 1998, p. 23). Students can also organize peer support networks for youth attacked by bullying or struggling to learn about the college application process as an antidote to the high school drop out/push out phenomenon. Or, as action steps, students produce plays, construct art installations, and organize community meetings to raise awareness about selected issues.

While these phases are explored in the three subsequent chapters, they need not be pursued in linear order. For example, I can imagine a citizen entering a process of social change with an action step and through that action step coming to name and explain a particular social problem. Picture a school administration setting up recycling bins around the school, inviting students to throw their trash in the appropriate bins. As students take action by disposing of their garbage accordingly, they *then* ask themselves, "Why is recycling necessary?" Following this question, these students would be inspired to pursue a project in which they study the value of recycling; name the problems of trash management, pollution, and global warming; and recognize the complexity of all the competing solutions to these problems—one of which is recycling. These students would then be armed with knowledge to propose a new, more far-reaching action step that seeks to transform their school's policy of paper use and energy consumption in general. Here, the students went from action, to problem identification and exploration, and back to action. This example shows how the phases involved in a civic literacy project—naming a social problem, studying it, and taking action—can be pursued recursively in various orders.

Along with this review of the major phases, I would also like to introduce civic literacy projects in reference to the words in their title—civic, literacy, and project. First, civic literacy projects are all civic because they involve students in a broad social sphere. They scaffold opportunities for civic engagement, defined as "behavior that addresses legitimate public matters" (Levine, 2007, p. 4). These behaviors include acts of community participation such as volunteering and fundraising, as well as political actions where citizens vote, protest, and canvass to express a point of view, often to influence the state (Levine, 2007). Participation in these political components of civic life involves engaging and questioning power and advocating for sustainable change for many. Civic projects enacted with youth can ask them to analyze and critique current policies, explore a diversity of opinions on public issues to determine which one to advance, and work with others to solve problems—processes that scaffold opportunities for them to interface with political structures and develop democratic patriotism (Westheimer, 2007).

The second word in the phrase "civic literacy projects" is literacy, highlighting the ways the projects ask students to be literate in reference to a broad array of texts. Students read books, websites, and even social situations. They compose print, visual, and oral texts to articulate their messages to varied audiences. They are able to use certain language when speaking with their family and other language with public officials. Such components of civic literacy projects frame students' literacy skills as encompassing far more than how well they comprehend a print, assigned text and therefore ask teachers and students to adopt an enlarged conception of literacy in comparison to what is traditionally perceived. In this traditional paradigm, people consider individuals as "literate" if they can read a preselected text that communicates a message with words, generally within a school-based context. Yet constructs of learner, text, and context have broadened as literacy scholars have taken increased interest in students' social and cultural realities (Moje, Dillon, & O'Brien, 2000). Teachers who adopt this broadened perspective know to look for and affirm the ways their students are literate when comprehending oral and visual texts, as well as print texts, that they encounter inside and outside of the school. When citizens use literacy skills in the civic sphere—one particular social context that exists inside and outside of school—they read, talk, write, and draw so as to engage in public life.

Finally, civic literacy projects are "projects" in that they are extended, yet time-bound, efforts for students and teachers to be explicit and intentional about their desire to take on social problems. They are not brief events disconnected from the bulk of the curriculum, such as short-term charity efforts, nor should they be equated with efforts to teach civic skills through routine classroom projects that do not focus on particular civic dilemmas. For example, civic skills might be fostered continually throughout the school year by assigning students jobs that ask them to take responsibility in their classroom community. Theoretically, as students learn to operate as a class by assuming roles such as attendance monitor or homework collector, they learn how to collaborate and be conscientious—skills that could help them pursue civically engaged lives. This book describes something different—time-bound, concrete, and robust projects through which students learn about and attack lived, social problems.

PURSUING CIVIC LITERACY PROJECTS—A CHALLENGING ROAD

Enacting civic literacy projects in schools can be challenging for many reasons. To begin with, schools traditionally position students as passive and require them to be responsive to teachers and other authorities (Tyack & Cuban, 1995). The expectation is for students to display obedience. Therefore, when enacting civic literacy projects, teachers face the perplexing task of subverting this norm by encouraging students to use their voices and try to make changes in their communities.

Representative of the trend of diminishing students' empowerment, schools have long been seen as sites to transmit a codified body of content knowledge that has stood the test of time—a process that sidesteps student interests in general and their civic insights in particular. Advocates for a core-knowledge approach (Adler, 1982; Hirsch, 1996) argue that curricular topics should be standardized and predetermined, and, in this way, teachers can ensure that equal expectations are set and that all students have access to challenging educational programs. This framework generally affirms the authority of teachers, who are positioned as the determinants of what knowledge the students receive.

Furthermore, textbooks and perceptions of what constitutes "official knowledge" work heavily to silence student voices, particularly those that are marginalized (Apple, 2000). Teachers feel pressured to cover what is deemed "official knowledge" and ignore students' perspectives that would question these constructs. Teaching a prescribed set of content leads to a banking style of education in which knowledge is deposited in students' minds and they are seen as passive recipients (Freire, 1970). Student voices are often dismissed or limited in their impact on classroom events—and curriculum is not based on students' particularized, local civic identities. Models of schooling that prioritize teacher authority and prescribed content knowledge are quite distinguishable from civic literacy projects, where youth experience agency and their civic interests influence what resources (e.g., articles, movies) are used in instruction.

Upholding teaching norms that prioritize content coverage, not student engagement, some teachers present standardized bodies of knowledge in civics classes by focusing on government processes—such as how a bill becomes a law—or parts of the Constitution. In such classes, teachers focus on "emphasizing the formal processes of national politics and treating government with academic detachment rather than exploring ways that students can personally engage" (Levine, 2011, p. 211). While there is value in studying such processes, teachers are pressured by the culture of schooling to separate students from authentic community issues and immerse them, instead, in book knowledge. Furthermore, when "formal processes" are emphasized, students learn about one tip of the civic iceberg. For example, in order for a bill to become a law, a tremendous amount of political organizing and lobbying has occurred, yet this knowledge is obscured. If students only study some surface details about politics, they are denied a meaningful civic education.

Teachers today also face the pressure of standardized tests. Scholars have agreed for some time that the role of schooling to prepare students for civic participation has been overshadowed by the emphasis on standards, testing, and accountability (Berman, 2004; Cochran-Smith & Lytle, 2006). Teachers and students, particularly those in low-income communities, are placed under close scrutiny to ensure that they are preparing for the test—a process which inherently ignores the students' lived experiences (Lipman, 2007). If preoccupied by the importance of content "coverage" and teaching to the test, teachers are likely to avoid or struggle to find a place for civic projects in their curricula.

Finally, civic projects invite conversation about controversial topics that are generally silenced in schools. Teachers commonly avoid topics on which there are multiple opinions playing out in the media and broad civic sphere. An explanation for this follows:

> Parents, school administrators, teachers, and students do not want schools to be turned into ideological boot camps, and they often mistakenly believe that the purposeful insertion of highly contentious political issues into the school curriculum is a step in that direction. (Hess, 2009b, pp. 69–70)

Teachers may also more simply be concerned with how others will react if they address a controversial topic.

A fear of controversy limits curricular conversation about a variety of issues. Drawing on reviews of literature, experiences in schools and with student teachers, and a questionnaire to student teachers, researchers found that topics related to sex, race, and religion were seen as either strictly taboo or moderately taboo for classroom discussion (Evans, Avery, & Pederson, 2000). Focusing on teachers' reluctance to talk about race, we can see how this reluctance would limit many civic conversations, including those about de facto segregated neighborhoods, tracking practices in schools, or discriminatory policing. Shutting down conversations about topics such as race and racism implies a shutting down of civic dialogue in general.

While I recognize the reality of these perennial challenges, I also argue that teachers can assume agency to enact civic projects with their students despite their initial concerns. Teachers who are knowledgeable about a rationale for youth civic engagement will feel more confident about their ability to engage students' civic identities.

A RATIONALE FOR YOUTH CIVIC ENGAGEMENT

Given the barriers teachers experience in regard to civic curriculum enactments, teachers must have clear reasons to make room for civic literacy projects in their classrooms. I present four such reasons below, and teachers can recursively draw on them when confirming the importance of their work in this area. They are interrelated and collectively build a rationale for teachers to embrace a social reconstructionist orientation to curriculum that frames curriculum as a means to teaching students how to participate in social change (Eisner, 1985; Kliebard, 1995). Aligned with a social reconstructionist vision of curriculum, teachers enact civic literacy projects that are generative in the following ways.

Civic Literacy Projects Promote a Strong Democracy

Civic literacy projects are good for democracy in that they position citizens in an attentive role in which they take responsibility for particular civic issues and advocate for changes that will help themselves and their neighbors (Levine, 2007). As citizens work together in these ways, they promote a "strong democracy," where they consider the common good along with their own personal interests (Barber, 2003, p. 25). Alternatively, citizens may choose to civically engage in ways that promote a "thin democracy," where they act to meet their individualistic and private needs (p. 3). In a thin democracy, citizens only claim what they want, while in a strong democracy, citizens determine what will be good for "us." Barber (2003) shares a relevant example:

> I may want a big, fast, lead fuel–powered automobile, but I may not be prepared to will into existence a world with polluted air, concrete landscapes, depleted energy resources, and gruesome high-way death tolls; and so as a citizen I may act contrary to my private preferences. (p. 201)

Civic literacy projects can prepare students to make similar judgments based on a broad social purview. Personal interests do not disappear—they are fruitfully addressed given a commitment to ensuring a good life for many and for years to come.

Despite the value of balancing attention to the individual and attention to society, U.S. society generally favors the first and emphasizes the rights of the individual (Parker, 2003): "Individualism is the dominant ideology of contemporary American life. It existed before our births; we were born into it and grew up and formed our ideas and values within it" (p. 56). In some ways, it is important that citizens advocate for their individual needs and interests, as people can often most effectively represent themselves.

Yet, with too much individualism, people put their blinders on to pervasive social dilemmas facing themselves and others, which will ultimately lessen their quality of life. In a strong democracy, members of society recognize their interconnectedness to others and advocate for a lasting justice for themselves as well as their local and global "neighbors." This book explores how schools can be places that welcome and support such active civic participation.

As history shows, there are many practices that citizens use to protect a strong democracy. At times, citizens prioritize dialoguing in their communities and conducting research to build a critical consciousness about the problems around them. Such work will ideally include deliberation, where citizens explore different approaches they could take to promote change. Other practices include use of electoral channels, where citizens direct their messages to individuals who have been elected to represent their constituencies. They communicate with their representatives through lobbying, petitioning, writing persuasively, and staging public debates. Finally, citizens use the streets, and the public sphere in general, as venues for speeches, performance, and distribution of information. Through these and other practices, citizens craft opportunities to communicate and advocate for lasting change. In civic literacy projects, educators and students recognize these possibilities and select viable ways to forward their social knowledge and messages.

The results of active civic participation are compelling. When many people engage civically, they are likely to view their public institutions (i.e., local government, schools) positively, suggesting that the institutions themselves work well in communities where there is wide and robust participation (Levine, 2007). Furthermore, broad participation seems to yield citizens' appreciation of the civic protections that inform their lives in a democracy.

Particularly encouraging is the finding that those who participate in politics or community affairs as teenagers have been seen to integrate civic understandings into their identity, fostering civic engagement into adulthood (Youniss, McLellan, & Yates, 1997). Therefore, the enactment of civic literacy projects serves democracy in the present and in the future. Youth are likely to continue to hold institutions accountable to multiple constituencies' needs if they have an experience of this sort in their earlier years.

Civic Literacy Projects Position Youth as Empowered Civic Actors

Greene (1995) challenges teachers to envision classrooms where each student "stirs to wide-awakeness, to imaginative action, and to renewed consciousness of possibility" (p. 43). Civic literacy projects aid in this vision as they instill a sense of empowered purpose in the students who recognize their work as important. Their "wide-awakeness" can begin when they feel alive with an inspiration to work on something that drives them, lights a fire under them. Civic, political problems can do just that, as they regularly make citizens feel angry, responsible, moved to learn and act.

Specifically, adolescents who complain that school is boring or disconnected from their lives can be motivated to engage in school projects that integrate their social concerns and give them entry into real-life political arenas (Bomer, 2004). This provides reason for teachers to address not only civic issues in general but controversial civic issues, because if these issues excite the general public and provoke strong opinions, they will excite youth as well. Furthermore, when teachers foster discussions of authentic controversial issues, they acknowledge to the students that young people are able to engage with the same civic issues as adults.

Teachers who enact civic literacy projects position students as agents, not passive recipients of knowledge. In this vision, teachers embrace the following call:

> As teachers, we can work to find ways to engage students with their own situations; we can pose problems that might allow them to consider their vivid and essential places in the world. In that way, in this corner of this school or classroom, in this unique place—in this open space we are constructing together—people will begin to experience themselves as powerful authors of their own narratives, luminous actors in their own dramas, the essential creators of their own lives. (Ayers & Ayers, 2011, p. 37)

Civic literacy projects ask students to critically reflect on their lives and society at large and then act on their reflections. They therefore stand as a vehicle to the student empowerment described in this passage and interrupt the traditional positioning of students as passive in school.

Civic literacy projects also interrupt a subtler trend in civic education of preparing students to use skills of democratic participation that they will fully embrace *later* as adults (Biesta, 2007). Using this rationale, teachers and students pursue projects that are more symbolic than authentic, justifying their decision by stating that youth can't pursue real action. Symbolic projects provide opportunities for students to engage in simulations of community board meetings, as opposed to attending the actual meetings, or compose grant applications or persuasive letters to government bodies without actually sending them. Questioning this rationale, Biesta (2007) argues that "education should not be seen as a space of preparation, but should be conceived as a space where individuals can act" and then pointedly questions, "How much action is actually possible in our schools?" (p. 759). When teachers and students ask themselves this and then create spaces in schools for students to use their voices with others in meaningful ways, civic agency is possible.

A caveat before concluding—teachers may be so dedicated to the empowerment of youth that they lean too heavily on the assumption that student knowledge and skill can guide the entire process. This is a flawed assumption. Students should have the chance to draw productively on the knowledge and skills of teachers and other mentors as important resources. Civic literacy projects should not be seen as exclusively "youth-led" as this "leaves unexamined the critical roles that adults can, and often do, play" (Kirshner, 2006, p. 40). With this understanding, teachers dedicate themselves to modeling particular civic skills, coaching students to adopt these skills, and then fading to the background as students exercise them—a process called "youth-centered apprenticeship" (p. 53). In turn, teachers share their authority with youth (Oyler, 1996).

Civic Literacy Projects Build Civic Knowledge and Skills

While agency is a crucial component of civic participation, it must be embraced thoughtfully and skillfully mirroring "enlightened political engagement" (Parker, 2003, p. 33). "Enlightened political engagement" combines two concepts: political engagement and democratic enlightenment. Through political engagement, citizens take action; they speak out in reference to issues that motivate them. Democratic enlightenment refers to the moral, emotional, and intellectual insight that informs this action. When citizens participate in enlightened political engagement, they engage in action that serves to uphold broad political and justice-oriented ideals that they embrace as a result of their learning. Here, action is taken from a thoughtful and skilled stance, one that was formed after deliberating on the multiple viewpoints at hand and identifying a particular audience or target for the action—two key steps of many. Civic literacy projects scaffold opportunities for the learning of critical civic knowledge and skill, learning that makes action "enlightened."

In regard to knowledge, civic literacy projects build students' awareness about the sociohistorical patterns of any one public matter (e.g., immigration reform, child labor, gentrification) and how their identified problem takes shape in society. When they analyze data and reports on a social problem, students' knowledge about the problem increases along with their expressions of activism (e.g., Lester, Ma, Lee, & Lambert, 2006). Importantly, they establish knowledge that helps them view problems with sensitivity and value justice for all. This can happen when they approach social problems from multiple vantage points and question purviews that ignore injustices or view them through an overly simplistic or distorted lens. For example, if enacting an antipoverty project, students can partner with coalitions that organize citizens living in poverty and, in speaking with the organizers and the members, learn about their needs and experiences. This will enable them to enter into civic dialogues about the dire hardships of the poor, critique trends of marginalizing them in society, and knowledgeably challenge the status quo.

In regard to skills, through civic literacy projects, students practice transferable skills that can be applied to many school projects. Civic literacy projects foster a variety of academic literacy skills, including the ability to comprehend and critically analyze texts, looking for whose voices are represented and whose voices are missing, and the ability to persuasively communicate messages through multiple mediums (e.g., public forums, newspaper editorials, websites). Students also learn skills specific to the endeavor of civic engagement. For example, they can identify allies, opponents, and targets and evaluate the potential strengths and weaknesses of action steps. Furthermore, when students grapple with controversial issues in the classroom, they can learn skills of deliberation (Hess, 2009b). In preparation for a deliberative discussion, teachers and students study multiple approaches to any one controversy and then dialogue with their peers on these possibilities. These are skills that citizens use when participating in a strong democracy, and they should be experienced in schools.

Students also have interests in focusing on skills and knowledge that *they* deem as important, interests that are likely to grow as they form opinions about what they need to know and do to be successful in their civic agenda. For example, students might see the value of launching a website to address their identified social problem if, through their studies, they determine that the issue is not getting enough public attention. In this case, the students would then work to develop the skills to do so. Students' interests are addressed in the curriculum as teachers create a context for students to practice the skills and build the knowledge that is meaningful to them. Whether the intent emerges from the teachers or the students, civic literacy projects are productively analyzed for the way they support the building of specific knowledge and skills.

Civic Literacy Projects Address Standards

Not only can civic literacy projects foster the development of students' knowledge and skill overall, they can provide opportunities for students to develop the knowledge and skills prioritized in various state and national standards. Teachers are strained under multiple norms of accountability, and standards—particularly the Common Core State Standards (CCSS) (National Governors Association Center for Best Practices, Council of Chief State School Officers, 2010)—currently occupy much of teachers' attention. Teachers might understandably claim that they are overly concerned about developing skills prioritized in the standards and that they have no time for discussions of current issues. However, if teachers set out to engage their students in meaningful inquiries and actions on relevant issues, they can find opportunities to align civic projects with the standards (Beach, Thein, & Webb, 2012). Indeed, students studying any one civic problem can read many texts on this problem, find the main ideas of these texts, and cite them in their writing and speaking—all standards-based skills. Furthermore, to the disappointment of core-knowledge advocates who believe that standards should specify content knowledge for each grade (i.e., Hirsch, 1996), standards generally name few specific topics that must be covered. Therefore, civic literacy projects, focusing on social problems related to poverty, discrimination, and so on, can be aligned with standards that emphasize general reading, writing, and speaking/listening skills.

Aligning standards with plans for civic engagement projects may feel like trying to speak in two languages at once. The standards might feel overly technical—focusing on discrete academic skills—and teachers experience them as a heavy obligation, given the way school administrators are requiring adherence to them and the high-stakes tests that are used to evaluate whether students are meeting them. In comparison, civic literacy projects could seem more open-ended and oriented as much around social skills as academic skills. Given this likely disconnect, below I aim to aid teachers as they face the challenging demands involved in working with the standards by pointing out possible connections between standards and civic literacy projects.

The importance of civic engagement is particularly clear in social studies standards, and social studies teachers need not work hard at building an alignment between civic literacy projects and their content-area standards. Social studies teachers are expected to "provide opportunities for learners to practice forms of civic discussion and participation consistent with the ideals of citizens in a democratic republic" (National Council for the Social Studies [NCSS], 2002, p. 35).

While generally less explicit about civic life, standards commonly addressed in English language arts can also provide a helpful road map to think about the forms of civic engagement students and teachers might prioritize in a civic literacy project. To illustrate, key components of a civic literacy project mirror English language arts standards published by the National Council of Teachers of English (NCTE) and the International Reading Association (IRA) (2009), as demonstrated in Epstein (2010). First, civic literacy projects scaffold opportunities for students to "conduct research on issues and interests by generating ideas and questions, and by posing problems" (Standard 7). Students read print and nonprint texts on topics including pollution and racial profiling and question how they are positioned in the texts, in relation to the problem, and in reference to what they can do about it. Second, students "employ a wide range of strategies as they write and use different writing process elements" (Standard 5). Civic literacy projects craft opportunities for them to create and revise work to articulate social messages in line with the interests of their audiences. Their messages might be shared in a print editorial in a newspaper or a speech delivered at a school board meeting, asking students to "adjust their use of spoken, written, and visual language" accordingly (Standard 4). Teachers can develop generative relationships between standards and students' civic interests and recursively draw on both within the curriculum.

This exercise, linking standards to particular phases of a civic literacy project, can also be done with the Common Core State Standards (CCSS). These standards similarly state the importance of reading and writing for particular purposes (e.g., finding the central idea of text and writing argumentative texts)—skills that are readily practiced during civic literacy projects. For example, Liz Boeser, a 12th-grade teacher, involved her students in a project in which they critiqued their school's Internet access policy; they felt that too many sites were unnecessarily blocked (Beach, Thein, & Webb, 2012). They engaged in many writing activities to define their stances on the issue of Internet access and then wrote position papers offering recommendations to their school administration. Their work structured ample opportunities for them to meet CCSS for writing, including for example, the first anchor standard for writing (Grades 6–12), that asks students to "write arguments to support claims in an analysis of substantive topics or texts, using valid reasoning and relevant and sufficient evidence."

The importance of Liz's work is summarized here:

> Rather than using the Common Core State Standards to provide a template for organizing curriculum standard by standard, Liz used meaningful issues and activities to create opportunities to engage in literacy practices that allowed students to meet the standards. (Beach, Thein, & Webb, 2012, p. 43)

Similarly, I encourage teachers to identify relevant, pressing social problems that affect and interest the students and then craft opportunities for the students to meet the standards while addressing these social problems. As teachers like Liz work to associate the projects with the standards, they can provide clear opportunities for students to read a range of texts and compose well-conceived print and oral pieces during civic literacy projects.

A TIMELINE OF CIVIC LITERACY

Teachers have acknowledged the value of civic literacy projects for over a century. Here, I offer a brief history of individuals and groups that have sought to protect and forward the understanding that schools can be sites of social change. The stories of these individuals and groups can sharpen teachers' understanding of what is possible in their classrooms, adding to the rationale presented above.

Social Reconstructionists

At the start of the 20th century, a debate emerged on the value of four approaches to curriculum: a humanist curriculum that would impart time-honored knowledge to youth; a student-centered curriculum, or developmentalist tradition, that would support each student's individual needs and interests; a scientific curriculum oriented around a series of particularized objectives that would prepare students to productively engage in the workforce; and a social meliorist curriculum that asked students to critique and improve society (Kliebard, 1995). Social reconstructionists were an offshoot of the social meliorists, as they wanted schools to further social and economic justice. Teachers, youth workers, parents, and many who care about how youth experience school have debated the benefits and drawbacks of these visions for curriculum for over 100 years. I enter this debate with this book that illustrates the power of social reconstructionist teaching—or teaching that promotes social change.

The social reconstructionists wanted youth to participate in the betterment of society and specifically promoted a form of collectivism that advocated for social mobility for groups of people, not solely privileged individuals. George S. Counts, a prominent social reconstructionist, critiqued scientific curriculum making for the way he believed it preserved the status quo, tracking students into roles within the existing social order (Kliebard, 1995). To counter this trend, he advocated that schools be sites for creative change. He wanted students to be taught to act for the improvement of society and was even seen to argue that schools should "unflinchingly indoctrinate students" to work for reform (Makler, 2004, p. 29). Towards this end, Counts (1932) called on teachers to cease acting in obedient ways to the structures that oversee them and conversely wield their power to create potential for a new social order.

Harold Rugg emerged as less radical than Counts in that he opposed the indoctrination of students yet was similarly committed to the creation of a more democratic society. Rugg wanted to teach students to be informed about social issues, to be able to rigorously discuss them, and to be motivated to civically participate. He envisioned schools where social problems—including those related to immigration, natural resources, education, and international relations—were to be tackled one at a time and studied in depth (Evans, 2007). I too advocate for projects that ask students to develop a deep understanding of social problems. Therefore, I present his story here in some detail.

Rugg argued that social science curriculum should be organized around social problems and not divided into subjects such as geography, civics, and history (Kliebard, 1995; Watras, 2004). To support this vision, he developed a series of texts through which students could learn to analyze social issues within the United States. First through a series of pamphlets and later through textbooks, students were presented with issues, and the instruction was meant to ask them to deliberate and exercise critical judgments in relation to them (Evans, 2007).

Rugg's work was a great accomplishment. Between 1929 and 1939, over one million textbooks and over two million accompanying workbooks were sold (Evans, 2007). This reflected a trend of the period, as there was a growing network of educators and researchers committed to infusing the curriculum with discussions of social issues. For example, during the 1930s, social studies journals published an increasing number of articles on the teaching of civic problems.

Rachel Davis DuBois stands as another example of an educator committed to addressing social realities of that time in the classroom. Between 1933 and 1936, she devised curriculum units on different immigrant groups (i.e., Chinese, Japanese, Jewish, Irish, etc.), aiming to prepare students to expand their notions of who was an American (Pak, 2004). She was inspired to do this work after witnessing discrimination as a high school teacher in New Jersey.

Despite this trend, Rugg's texts went from being the bestselling texts ever published to being attacked by conservative groups. The American Legion, upholding a tradition of suppressing what they saw as subversive un-American activity, played an active role ensuring that schools did not use the texts (Evans, 2007). The books—which arguably presented human rights as more important than private property—were framed as an attack on capitalism. Critics also called the texts un-American because of the way the books indicated that there were groups of people that were poorly represented within the U.S. democracy. Finally, critics believed students should not study multiple perspectives and instead should be taught one "correct" version of issues and history (Makler, 2004). In this context, members of school boards and civic organizations launched complaints demanding that Rugg's books be removed from schools. Rugg's censors led an insistent, anti-intellectual campaign, diminishing book sales and this civic approach to education. And, from the 1940s and into the 1960s, supplemental subjects, including social studies, were fearfully framed as potential opportunities for teachers to discuss socialism and communism (Spring, 1989). These trends contributed to a lasting cultural taboo against discussion of social issues in the curriculum.

Contrary to Rugg's critics, those committed to the teaching of human rights and multiple perspectives on history and civic problems will see Rugg's work as admirable. Indeed, Evans (2007) calls on educators to use Rugg's story "not only as a well-spring of inspiration, but as a source of ideas for practical action, praxis, with the aim of social improvement" (p. 293). Rugg's critique of the curriculum as not adequately preparing students for civic dialogue is still relevant, and teachers can draw on his ideas to imagine an issues-centered curriculum that asks students to confront timely social questions.

The social reconstructionist vision gained popularity again in the 1960s when a vocal movement for social justice rose up. During this time, there was a broad willingness to question the status quo and embrace change— a willingness that led social studies educators to consider how to address issues of social unrest with their students (Howard, 2004; Mullen, 2004). The National Council for the Social Studies (NCSS) Curriculum Guidelines published in 1971 illustrate this new direction (Mullen, 2004). The guide- lines stated that the social studies curriculum should emphasize civic prob- lems—such as war, racism, pollution—and students should be involved in resolving them. While sample problems were identified, the guidelines also emphasized that students should be consulted about what would be mean- ingful for them to study. The document positioned youth as knowledgeable about social concerns and as potential activists.

In the 1960s, Paulo Freire also began experimenting with a pedagogy that involved students in the investigation of their social positions, and he presented a call for social change through education in *Pedagogy of the Oppressed* (Freire, 1970). Referencing his work with adult learners, he ad- vocated for a form of literacy instruction grounded in students' political identities that could invoke change-making dialogues and help students problematize unjust aspects of their lives: "As an event calling forth the critical reflection of both the learners and educators, the literacy process must relate *speaking the word* to *transforming reality*" (Freire, 1985, p. 51). He explained that literacy instruction should be based around "generative words," chosen for their phonemic qualities as well as the extent to which they address students' political, cultural, and social realities (Freire, 1973). His views, referenced throughout this book, can influence teachers today as they craft ways for students to speak, read, and write about their political and social situations.

The efforts of educators such as Harold Rugg, Rachel Davis DuBois, and Paulo Freire, as well as the collaborative decisions of social studies educators who argued that students robustly address social problems in schools, signify the historical presence of a social reconstructionist orientation to curriculum. Their stories present points of inspiration and questions of how this work can be most effectively pursued. Teachers and scholars continue to pursue these questions and search for ways to engage their students in the civic world.

The Persistence of a Civic, Justice-Oriented Vision for Schools

Scholarship brings to light teachers more recently scaffolding opportunities for students to analyze social ills and address them. These opportunities are assigned many labels, including social action projects, social justice education, youth civic engagement, and the historically situated term, social reconstructionist teaching. More critical than their labels is the way these projects provide inspiring and instructive messages about the potential of youth to meaningfully, civically engage in educational settings. For example, high school students in Tar Creek, Oklahoma, worked with school and community leaders to investigate the environmental devastation that arose when nearby abandoned, unused mine shafts were left unsealed, causing widespread lead poisoning and disease in their community (Kesson & Oyler, 1999; Oyler, 2012). Their studies led them to explore citizens' movements, including the use of boycotts, petitions, and lobbying, and how the creation of jobs might be prioritized over environmental protections. Ultimately, they composed writing and conducted tours of environmentally challenged sites to raise awareness about the hazardous conditions of their immediate surroundings.

Elementary-age students engage in this work as well. Katherine Bomer's 4th- and 5th-grade students formed coalitions around common social concerns, researched these concerns, and then created texts that they sent to authentic, public audiences pressing for change (Bomer & Bomer, 2001). For example, the "Violence by Police" coalition wrote letters to the police commissioner and the then-mayor of New York City, Rudolph Giuliani, about police brutality. Their letter to the mayor included the following text: "We are writing to you because we know you have the power to change the way police are using their utilities against people who have rights" (Bomer & Bomer, 2001, p. 148). They worked to develop a tone in their writing that would allow it to be well received by their readers, one skill of many that was taught through mini-lessons and other teacher input.

Schultz (2008) depicts 5th-graders working on one collaborative project to get a new school building. Their school suffered from poor heat, no gymnasium or cafeteria, bullet holes in the windows, and other problems. They read about inequities in urban schooling to place their school's inadequacies in a larger sociocultural frame; met with politicians and journalists to present their views; and composed letters, petitions, and oral presentations advocating for their cause. The students in these classes were highly motivated to get involved in school projects that involved political agency.

Texts created in the Rethinking Schools publishing house consistently discuss how to teach for social change and the value of such instruction (e.g., Bigelow, Christensen, Karp, Miner, & Peterson, 1994; Bigelow, Harvey, Karp, & Miller, 2001), and civically engaged teaching is a central focus of *Rethinking Schools* magazine. For example, a recent volume of the magazine includes an article on a high school teacher who involved his students in a unit on mass incarceration and the long-term consequences citizens face when they are convicted of a felony (Peck, 2013). The students read various texts on these problems, including excerpts from *The New Jim Crow* (Alexander, 2010)—a powerful book detailing how trends of mass incarceration perpetuate historically entrenched forms of racism. They also enacted a role-play where they embodied the perspectives of formerly incarcerated people, law enforcement officials, employers and business leaders, and others. Finally, they wrote letters to their local representatives expressing their views on a statewide "ban the box" bill that would free formerly incarcerated people from the obligation to check a box asking them "Have you ever been convicted of a felony?" on initial job applications. While the majority of students supported this bill, others opposed it, and all of the youth were guided through rich instruction to help them understand this pressing issue. The above cases depict teachers provoking students' thinking and action about social problems, illustrating how this pedagogical approach is alive in today's schools.

Additionally, scholars have pursued inquiries to explore intriguing nuances of civic work. A key example is Westheimer and Kahne's (2004) study that exposes the difference between civic work that highlights community engagement and that which involves structural critique. They explain how skills of community engagement were fostered when high school students from Madison County, located in a suburban/rural East Coast community, studied public matters, such as the work of fire and rescue departments, and created reports of their findings that were delivered to their local county's board of supervisors. During their 12th-grade government class, these students interacted with government agencies, and many students tangibly affected their community. At the end of this project, the students reported a heightened belief that they could be effective leaders and a greater commitment to community involvement. They did not, however, consider structural issues or questions of systemic injustice, such as the relationship between race or class and the topics they were addressing.

In contrast, another project that the same researchers studied was the Bayside Students for Justice curriculum that included more structural critique—such as a study of the social, political, and economic components of child labor (Westheimer & Kahne, 2004). Following this curriculum, enacted as part of a 12th-grade social studies class in an urban high school on the West Coast, the Bayside students showed increases in their ability to explore structural explanations for poverty and a desire to engage in politics. The Madison students, focused solely on community engagement, showed no change in these areas. The Bayside students' learning differed from that of the Madison students in that they exhibited a desire to question injustices at their root and push for social change through politics, not their communities. Indeed, Bayside students showed no increase in their knowledge about community resources, and their sense of being effective community leaders remained unchanged. In sum, the Madison project fostered skills of community engagement and the Bayside project the skill of critiquing the social structures that undergird society. Such research illustrates the different ways that teachers can position students as active citizens, concerned about society, and raises questions of how to give attention to both community engagement and structural critique.

This book draws on cases such as the ones above to illustrate how teachers involve their students in civic life in varied ways. They enact "pedagogy designed around the real," welcoming authentic social and political issues into the curriculum (Oyler, 2012, p. 48). Throughout the text, I communicate what I have learned about their efforts so to provide entry points for other teachers into this endeavor.

WHERE TO START?

Teachers' rationales about the importance of civic literacy projects are likely to grow as they enact the projects with their students, so the remainder of the chapter outlines different ways for this work to begin. First, if teachers are accustomed to crafting frameworks, or unit plans, for the units they teach prior to introducing them to the students, they should begin by crafting such a plan for the enactment of a civic literacy project. In their planning processes, teachers can establish long-term goals and essential questions, or open-ended questions about the central topic of the unit, determine the knowledge and skills they hope students to master over the course of the unit, and brainstorm different learning activities that will allow students to meet the identified goals (Wiggins & McTighe, 2005). Embedded in their plan should be opportunities to integrate the students' emergent civic interests and intents. Students can play important roles in choosing what social problem they address, how they study it, and what action step they pursue.

For example, in a civic literacy project on child labor, imagine teachers and students pursuing the following essential questions: "What are the factors that contribute to the use of child labor?" "What are the experiences of child laborers?" and "What actions can I take to address the problems involved in child labor?" Multiple learning activities would support their work on these questions; they could interview former child laborers and read about advocacy groups that organize against child labor—just to name two options. In one elementary classroom, similar activities led up to the production of a play for the school community on the plight of child laborers (see Epstein & Oyler, 2008; Rogovin, 1998). This brief outline of a unit on child labor entails the essential questions, related learning activities, and a summative product. Identifying these components of a civic literacy project is a helpful place for teachers to start to conceive of the shape of the endeavor.

Teachers might create a framework for a project independently, perhaps during the summer, or they might collaborate with other teachers to plan one or many civic literacy projects to be used in their school. Additionally, teacher candidates, or preservice teachers, can work with their teacher mentors and university faculty to create plans for civic literacy projects while learning the art of curriculum design. This process of unit design for civic literacy projects is outlined in more detail in Chapter 6.

A related way for teachers to start planning for a civic literacy project is to look for readily accessible opportunities to ignite a civic literacy project in their school. First, schools routinely organize special service-learning days or charity projects. While students should ultimately do more than participate in 1-day events or collect charitable donations, these types of events can be productively framed as entry points for civic literacy projects. For example, if a school is collecting money for an organization supporting people living with HIV/AIDS, this could lead to a larger unit on the fight against HIV/AIDS. During the unit students could research how individuals with HIV/AIDS get their health needs met and government and health officials' stances on HIV/AIDS research. Their action steps might include creating a book that documents oral histories of people living with HIV/AIDS and distributing the book to policymakers for them to better understand these experiences. Through this work, students and teachers can extend a charity campaign in a way that asks youth to recognize the deep-rootedness of a social problem and engage in action that seeks to affect the problem in the long term.

Also, the writing curriculum can be framed as a starting point, as middle and high school humanities curricula ask students to compose writing pieces that could be tailored to incorporate and address civic questions. Common examples of this are the argumentative essay or the research paper. Students can write pieces on issues that impact their lives and distribute their products to authentic audiences. For example, English or social studies teachers could ask students to research and compose argumentative pieces articulating their views on policies affecting charter schools or on the creation of one in their neighborhood. Then, they might read excerpts from them at community meetings held to review charter school proposals.

The reading curriculum or an examination of the assigned content-area texts is another potential starting point, as students routinely read texts in the traditional school curriculum that provoke their thinking about civic issues. A literature unit anchored on *The Grapes of Wrath* (Steinbeck, 1939) can include a civic literacy component in which students study the economic recession that began in 2007 and communicate their viewpoints on efforts to curtail unemployment and poverty. A history unit raising questions about national security can include a study of the recent wars in Iraq and Afghanistan and ask students to read about the current policy negotiations of these military endeavors. Teachers can pursue the formal curriculum, consider "official knowledge" (Apple, 2000) or the canon, and create space for the exploration of pressing social issues. Overall, these suggestions ask teachers to be "on the lookout" for ways to draw on the existing curriculum and involve students in timely, civic dialogues.

Finally, at times, teachers will identify a starting point by naming a pressing or painfully obvious civic problem facing the students. If the students' school is likely to be imminently shut down and, in front of the school, there are continuous rallies of people seeking to protect it, this can provoke teachers to involve the students in the debate. Or students might air concerns about a specific issue in the classroom, and these concerns can be drawn out and addressed through a civic literacy project. The pressing nature of the issue might inspire a teacher to "massage" or set aside any prescribed pacing calendar, based on required topics or book titles, and make room for the study of an emergent civic problem. Specifically when working with administration, teachers can cite the points above outlining a rationale for civic literacy projects and, depending on the flexibility of their curricular obligations, offer that they work in collaboration with school staff to ensure that the standards or other requirements are met. Ultimately, the emergence of a timely issue should be seen as a rich opportunity to develop a civic literacy project.

Civic literacy projects hold great promise. They involve students and teachers in a process of assuming thoughtful civic stances and taking action. They play a role upholding democracy while scaffolding opportunities for students to learn transferable skills such as critical reading, persuasive writing, and deliberation. The remainder of this book offers suggestions and insight on how to make them happen. Specifically, the next three chapters detail how teachers and students can engage in key components of civic literacy projects: problem identification, problem exploration, and action.

CHAPTER 2

Problem Identification

You are at a party. Someone says she has been busy working on a social action committee, a community-organizing project, or a civic project in school. You ask: "What's your focus? What's your issue?" She could respond by naming a whole range of public matters such as "affordable housing," "allocation of tax monies for global humanitarian aid," "curriculum reform in the local schools," or "local environmental protections." With the abundance of civic problems to choose from, this chapter aims to guide teachers through the process of identifying problems to focus on during their work with students. In Chapter 1, I briefly outlined what I see as the three phases of civic literacy projects: problem identification, problem exploration, and action. In this chapter, I explicate the first in this list—problem identification—in more detail.

When educators and students enter the phase of problem identification, they name festering problems in their communities, countries, and world and ultimately select one problem or a group of problems to address throughout the project. They can take community walks, participate in open discussions, and examine video and photographs to help in this process. To ensure that problem identification is meaningful for the students involved, teachers will invite them to share their own experiences, and their voices will inform the class's decision of what problems to take on. This validates student voice as opposed to bypassing it and requiring students to address predetermined social problems or exclusively learn about standardized political principles that do not reflect student interests.

The chapter opens with short vignettes exhibiting the unique ways each of the four anchor cases (see Chapter 1 for their introductions) engaged in problem identification. Then, I explore a common theme illustrated in the vignettes—the value of supporting youth to communicate their own stories, opinions, and knowledge when naming social problems. The chapter concludes with a review of three strategies teachers can use to identify civic dilemmas that relate to students' experiences and insights.

PICTURES OF PROBLEM IDENTIFICATION

This section presents four vignettes of educators and youth identifying social problems to focus on during their civic literacy projects. Each of their processes was different. In one class, students mainly pursued independent research to identify social problems while another class prioritized whole-group discussion to air shared concerns. For some classes, the process was lengthy. For others, it was short. While in one case, the educators took the lead in presenting a central problem to address, in others they put the onus on the students to find a problem of interest to them. I present the following stories so as to illustrate the multiple approaches teachers can take when challenged to select one or more problems that reflect the students' lives and concerns.

Social Justice Writing Assignment

Scott Rosner, an 8th-grade English and social studies teacher in a combined middle and elementary school called The Norman Rockwell School, was committed to crafting opportunities for his primarily Black and Latino/a students to question what they saw around them. Specifically, he wanted his students to select social problems to study and write about in a spring unit he called "the social justice writing assignment." He imagined the students using their writing to advocate for change in regard to problems of their choosing. Thus, one of their first assignments was to make observations of critical social problems impacting their homes and community, as well as efforts to positively address these problems, and record them in their notebooks. Scott told the students to "stay close to home" and "describe something you have seen"—directions designed to elicit students' insights about their neighborhood characterized by its low socioeconomic status. They described public matters including air pollution, teen pregnancy, and poor trash collection.

Scott also introduced texts that discussed a range of additional social problems and asked students to write and speak about them. He read aloud selections from *Voices of a People's History of the United States* (Zinn & Arnove, 2004), sharing stories of individuals from American history who have fought for various forms of social change, and pointed their attention to multiple civic issues during their independent reading of *The New York Times*, delivered each morning to their class. During these lessons, Scott addressed issues related to immigration reform, health standards in the meat industry, the treatment of the military serving the United States abroad, and other topics. Students also worked in the computer lab to conduct searches on the Internet to learn more about problems that piqued their interest.

At the end of the multiweek problem identification process, each student self-selected one social problem on which he or she would focus for the remainder of the assignment. The problems were varied, and they represented realities of the students' own city (e.g., high rent in their neighborhood) as well as those more global in nature (e.g., the AIDS epidemic in Africa). Scott offered questions to guide their selection process: "If you chose that as the seed idea for writing for social justice, what would you write about? What would you try to change? Who would be your target?" In turn, even as the students were identifying problems to address, he pushed them to envision their action steps and the "targets," or audiences, they would aim to reach.

Safe Sex Health Project

The facilitators of a civic literacy project in The Leadership Academy positioned students with a similar level of empowerment during the problem identification process. Like Scott, they wanted the students to choose their own focus. Specifically, the central facilitator of this project, Tanisha McGuire, wanted the 9th-grade students to identify problems in their life and develop skills to deal with them. She was employed by a nonprofit organization called Urban Youth and visited The Leadership Academy once a week during the students' advisory period to enact the civic project. The small high school, servicing primarily Black and Latino/a students, structured this advisory period as a place for students to receive support in their content-area classwork and pursue projects, such as a civic literacy project, that would develop their leadership. Tanisha worked closely with other cofacilitators and two classroom teachers who were otherwise responsible for the advisory periods.

At the start of the project, in order to air the students' concerns, the facilitators and teachers organized an open forum where students could present problems that bothered them. One teacher, Kris Stevenson, explained: "We didn't come to them with the ideas. We just came with the questions." Tanisha shared the program's intention: "We try to have them self-select and do the things that they are most interested in doing." They felt strongly that the project should be guided by the students' interests, not theirs.

And a clear student interest emerged. At one point, a student said that he and his peers didn't know the "right" age to have sex. Then, as Kris described, "Everyone jumped on that bandwagon [getting involved in the conversation]." They complained that they were not taught enough about sex education in school and that they "didn't want to catch anything." Students also shared other social concerns, unrelated to sex education, yet the final list presented problems mainly related to sexual health and drug abuse. Near the end of the period, Kris suggested that they select their focus by majority vote, and the majority selected sexual health. In comparison to the social justice writing assignment, the problem identification process was completed in a singular meeting during which the students voted on one problem to work on collectively. Yet, in both classes, the educators gave the students opportunities to have a say.

Race Awareness After-School Program

The race awareness after-school program was oriented around one, broad predetermined problem: racial discrimination. Paid staff members of Beyond Today, a nonprofit organization, created a 10-session curriculum that asked students to critique racial discrimination and the related, lasting forms of segregation in society. The staff was driven by the urgency of the issue, as they observed de facto segregated schools running in close geographic proximity to each other, containing students who would likely never meet. In cities, White students with financial privileges often attend private schools, and many public schools in rather affluent neighborhoods are under-resourced and primarily attended by Black and Latino/a students (Noguera, 2003). The diverse nature of cities can theoretically provide multiple opportunities for people to dialogue across difference, but this rarely occurs. Beyond Today aimed to address this concern.

Specifically, the after-school program was organized to bring students from de facto segregated schools together to learn about each other, current and historical trends of discrimination, and how forms of discrimination have been resisted. It was advertised through their schools, and ultimately 4th- and 5th-grade students from three distinct schools signed up. They formed a multiracial community of White, Black, and Latino/a students. They met monthly, gathering at least once in each of their schools and in other rented spaces over the weekends.

While the overarching problem of racial discrimination was predetermined, the students were supported to express their own connections to it. For example, in one activity, students looked at a map that portrayed the segregated racial demographics of their neighborhoods, along with other texts about their neighborhoods, and answered questions such as "What did you learn about who lives in your city? Why do different people live in different places?" As the youth reacted to the texts, students spoke of their perceptions of and experiences with racial segregation and the value of "mixing it up" or becoming friends with people of different races. They were also asked to make observations about each of the neighborhoods and schools they visited, which occasionally prompted the students to acknowledge the differences between the schools' facilities. For example, the students of color exclaimed "No fair!" when they saw the gym and cafeteria at the school the White students attended. The students' lives were impacted by issues of inequity, brought to light through the after-school curriculum.

Park Project

Before the park project began, 7th-grade teachers in an urban elementary and middle school called The Fields School brainstormed for weeks about problems that might form the central focus of their civic literacy project. They wanted to ensure that the problem be one that would interest the students. Deanne Holly, the English and social studies teacher who led the project, said that ideally, "it should come from the bottom up" and that it would be important to "have the kids pick the issue that they want to talk about, like pollution, or maybe gangs." She considered continuing a civic project they had begun the year before on the expansion of a nearby university into their community populated by many poor residents of color. The students, who were racially and economically representative of the community, had already begun to develop knowledge on this topic and shared diverse opinions about the impact of the expansion.

However, before Deanne and Lucy Oaks, the special education coteacher, reignited the university expansion project, students informed them that the budget of a local park was being cut. In the park, signs were posted notifying residents that, given the proposed budget cuts, the visiting hours of the park were soon to be shortened and that the outdoor pool would remain closed through the summer. Also, neighborhood residents set up a booth in front of the park asking park goers to sign a petition to restore the park budget. These signs and the petition caught the attention of two students, who then brought petitions they had collected at the park to their classroom. Deanne and Lucy thought to put this problem at the heart of the project because they felt it would really excite the students.

To confirm their hunch, they organized a lesson where they presented the news of the budget cuts and then asked the students to walk around the room and, through questioning, find another student who felt the same way about the cuts as they did. Following this lesson, they were convinced that the majority of the class opposed the proposed cuts. From there on, their civic literacy project was focused on the issue of the park budget.

Reading Across the Cases

In some ways, the youth and educators in all four cases tackled the process of choosing a problem for their project differently. Scott prioritized independent decisionmaking, allowing each student to choose his or her own focus. Tanisha organized a singular lesson involving communal dialogue about problems in the community, which surfaced the students' interest in sex education. The Beyond Today facilitators presented a problem—racial discrimination and segregation. They witnessed this problem impacting the students' schooling experiences and then asked students to identify their own connections to it. Deanne and Lucy followed the lead of two students concerned about a park budget and then crafted an activity to gauge the interests of the rest of the class. Clearly, problem identification can unfold in a variety of ways. I encourage teachers to consider how these models may be adapted for their own classrooms.

However, one component of these projects is common: They all addressed social problems that directly related to the students' lives or provoked the students' interests. Each problem was associated with the motivations, knowledge, and concerns of the students. The next section explains why selecting a problem of this ilk is important.

INTEGRATING STUDENTS' CIVIC KNOWLEDGE AND INTERESTS

Civic education projects optimally address social and political issues that generate high student interest (Parker, 2003), and those issues vary depending on what social, economic, and political conditions are impacting the students' communities. For some students, a pressing civic topic may be immigration reform, as their parents or loved ones are in danger of being deported. Others may be motivated to craft an antibullying policy for their school that currently does not have one and in which there are complaints of bullying. There is an unending list of social problems, but students will connect to and affirm some more than others. Civic curricula that are "decentralized and tailored to local school populations" make use of students' comparative viewpoints and honor students' knowledge, compared to those that teach standardized sets of political principles and practices (Gimpel & Lay, 2006, p. 13).

Such decentralized civic curricula emerge when students express their authentic concerns and ideals. This participation enables teachers to validate the students' experiences. Furthermore, the class can then choose to focus on social problems that reflect the students' lives. To support teachers to meet this goal, below I offer a brief discussion of how students' civic knowledge gets misunderstood and, to counter this, examples of research and teaching that validates students' civic experiences and insights.

Minimizing Students' Civic Knowledge

Unfortunately, civic educators in the United States often bypass or minimize their students' civic knowledge, which could play a helpful role in determining the problem that students and teachers choose to address. An international study, drawing on data from 200 civic-related teachers, shows that teachers in the United States were most unlikely to want to negotiate with students about what is taught in comparison to teachers from Norway,

Finland, Belgium, and Portugal, who were most likely to want to negotiate with students (Torney-Purta, Barber, & Richardson, 2005). This finding
frames U.S. teachers as reticent to address students' personal and communal
civic interests. It also reflects a broader concern that teachers face about
how students' "funds of knowledge"—the knowledge that students gain
through their own cultures and personal experiences—are integrated into
the classroom in general (Moll, Amanti, Neff, & Gonzalez, 1992). Scott,
Tanisha, the Beyond Today facilitators, and Deanne and Lucy stand as
notable examples of educators who addressed students' experiences with
social problems. Yet, more often than not, students' funds of knowledge are
not integrated.

When civic education projects are not tailored to the students' lives and
interests, units will likely emphasize a uniform set of facts about the political
system, such as how the Senate compares to the House of Representatives.
This foundational knowledge has value and can inform students' participation. However, if civics is exclusively taught with a form of academic
detachment, students are not supported to engage in civic life to improve
their own communities. Or a teacher might choose a civic problem to address without considering the social realities of the students and, in turn, ask
students to dedicate themselves to a problem that has little bearing on them.
This is likely to reduce student motivation and paint an inaccurate picture
of how and why people get civically engaged.

Just as students' voices are bypassed in the classroom, their interests and
abilities are also often misrepresented in education scholarship. Researchers
generally use tests to assess students' civic abilities and compose questions
aiming to evaluate particular skills and knowledge that they deem important in civic life (Rubin, 2007). They focus on quantifiable activities such
as likeliness to vote or frequency of reading the newspaper. Then, using
questionnaires, they survey youth on these behaviors. While these methods
surface some useful information, they can only evaluate certain testable behaviors, and other potentially important data do not emerge. For example,
a student might not read the newspaper but is commonly involved in dinner-
table discussions about the need for police reform. Yet, the survey might not
prompt him about the frequency of such discussions, and even if it does, he
might not acknowledge their impact on him unless asked about specific topics that his family addresses. In turn, through exclusive use of such surveys,
teachers and others are provided with an incomplete picture of students'
civic experiences. Studies dominated by quantitative data obtained through
tests and surveys, and in general all those with close-ended designs, "risk
blinding us to the variety of forms of engagement that young people may be
exploring" (Flacks, 2007, p. 79).

The qualitative, ethnographic methods of interview and observation
can provide needed details about how youth actually understand social

problems and seek to improve their communities and society. In using these methods, researchers talk with and observe youth during their normal days so to identify how they are civically engaged. The study of civics and citizenship education has been dominated by survey methods, and so the "diverse methodological toolkit" of anthropology, including its use of ethnographic methods, has much to contribute (Levinson, 2005, p. 336). The students in the park project might not have checked a box on a survey indicating their belief that petitions can be used to influence politicians or their interest in state budgets. However, when observed in their own community, students were motivated to collect petitions and speak to their classroom teachers about them.

Flacks (2007) further illustrates the importance of permitting youth to speak for themselves when describing their civic identity, as opposed to checking off boxes on a survey. He spotlights a study, intended to gather data on college students' civic engagement, that asked participants to both answer open-ended questions and a series of what he calls "forced-choice, close-ended questions" (p. 68). Their open-ended responses surfaced an important critique of the close-ended part of the survey; the participants complained about the question that asked them to identify with particular social groups (e.g., partygoers, intellectuals, liberal students, conservative students). They claimed that it was inappropriate to assume that these groups existed and participants would want to identify with particular groups. Other parts of the survey indicated their awareness of the politics of race, gender, class, and nationality, yet their resistance to easily affiliate with certain cultural groups suggests their interest in "transcending such fault lines" and their desire "to forge novel forms of social and political solidarity" (p. 78). If this finding surfaced in a classroom, the teacher might be encouraged to introduce students to a wide range of social problems that relate to the students' community as well as those in bordering neighborhoods, allowing students to form varying alliances with communities throughout the area.

Ultimately, the students' critique of the survey highlights the importance of allowing youth to speak for themselves, rather than only offering them a predetermined list of possible answers (Flacks, 2007). This message is applicable for researchers and classroom teachers alike. Without opportunities for the students to share their own affiliations and civic identities, students' experiences are evaded. In comparison, when they are surfaced, teachers can think more carefully about the types of social problems students may be interested in pursuing.

Valuing Students' Civic Knowledge

Some researchers are indeed talking with students so as to learn about their civic insights. One study involved interviews with secondary students from immigrant backgrounds and those from "dominant-culture" families who were participating in a summer program emphasizing citizenship (Myers & Zaman, 2009, p. 2592). While the immigrant students favored "universal positions" that emphasized all people's shared rights and the dominant-culture students more often sought to balance their national and global interests (p. 2615), over half of the students took different positions on particular subcategories within these spectrums. In response to such data, teachers can design ways to support students to negotiate their varied interests and find common causes. Another study involved youth expressing how they experience citizenship in their lives (Hart, 2009). When interviewed, a diverse pool of youth spoke of age-based discrimination—an important issue that they might address through a civic engagement project—and also their coveting of greater inclusion in an adult civic world. These findings reveal how interview-based methodologies can surface valuable details about youth civic identity, and that youth have important insights that can inform civic literacy projects.

Like certain researchers, some educators also work closely with youth to help them name and act on their civic values and concerns (see Kwon, 2008; Rubin, Hayes, & Benson, 2009; Schultz, 2008). Similar to the four cases presented at the start of chapter, in select classes and programs, youth address problems that they identify and that characterize their lives. For example, Kwon's research portrays teenage Asian and Pacific Islander youth naming the unfair treatment they experience at schools and organizing an advocacy campaign calling for school reform. Working with the support of a community-based youth collaborative, they collected 487 complaint forms in six high schools and eight junior high schools. The results were analyzed to determine how the youth felt their experience in schools was being compromised. Next, the teenage activists sought to persuade their superintendent to respond to the grievances and "require teachers to hand out a written grading policy; unlock bathrooms during passing periods; [and] include a lesson plan in the social studies curriculum for all middle schools and high schools on student rights, which includes information on the complaint process," among other demands (Kwon, 2008, p. 70). Ultimately, the superintendent spoke at a press conference about his intention to adhere to their demands and expressed pride in their work.

This study shares an inspiring example of what can happen when educators engage the concerns of youth. When youth share their experiences and knowledge, their civic interests become clear. These details can then signify what problems they should address through the curriculum. And, ultimately, when students address their authentic concerns, they can create change in *their* lives.

Teachers face a special and demanding challenge if they are enacting civic literacy projects with students whose experiences have taught them that they are not protected or valued within their country's civic structure.

In one study, this was found to be the case for urban youth of color in comparison to their White affluent peers (Rubin, 2007). During interviews and in-class discussions, the youth of color more often noted a "disjuncture" between the civic ideals of liberty and justice and their own life stories, in comparison to the White youth involved in the study (p. 461). For example, one African American 8th-grade student shared a story where the police searched through her house to look for her cousin, despite her "right to privacy." Students who experience such disjunctures question whether civic structures can truly work for them, as they feel mistreated by those who are supposed to keep them safe.

In response to students who identify disjunctures between civic ideals and their own experiences, Rubin (2007) argues that educators need to engage with the students about the disjunctures, provide a forum for analyzing them, and enact instruction that scaffolds the skills and knowledge they will need to navigate them. In this way, teachers acknowledge students' unique civic identities, welcome their thoughts into the classroom, and design instruction to help them negotiate their concerns. Whether surfacing disjunctures or other viewpoints, information about students' authentic fears and interests is essential for teachers to know so that they can help students find a place for themselves in civic life.

To conclude, efforts to identify and center students' authentic experiences are to be valued for a number of reasons during the problem identification phase of civic literacy projects and beyond. First, when teachers take students' ideas and experiences seriously, students will see that their voices, and their peers' voices, matter. Students will be more willing to become involved in classroom events, and their stories and ideas will generatively add to the information available for analysis (Lensmire, 1998). Second, teachers' practices are also enhanced, as they can gain the students' trust and learn valuable information about their students to integrate into the curriculum (Oyler, 1996). Third, when dialogue is built around students' stories, students can be positioned with the agency to act and improve their own life situations (Freire, 1970). For all these reasons, teachers should look for opportunities to draw on students' pressing concerns when addressing civic problems in the classroom.

PEDAGOGY FOR PROBLEM IDENTIFICATION
THAT VALUES STUDENT EXPERIENCES

Given the importance of taking students' experiences seriously in the problem identification phase of civic literacy projects, teachers are left to query what pedagogical moves will surface students' civic interests and knowledge. To start, educators must have an interest in sharing authority and feel comfortable doing so with students. In classrooms with shared authority, sometimes students take leadership roles, and other times teachers lead the way with the students' following (Oyler, 1996). There is a constant dance where every member of the classroom—students and teachers—acts with authority at different times and in different ways.

If teachers share authority, they are more likely to create spaces for student voice in the classroom. Such environments and the interactive class activities such as group-work that are commonly seen in them provide forums for the airing of students' ideas and enable students to build civic knowledge. Indeed, in a study that surveyed youth to understand the factors that led to their civic knowledge, not surprisingly, studying political topics in the classroom and experiencing an "open climate" in which to discuss them related positively and significantly to higher civic knowledge (Torney-Purta, Barber, & Wilkenfeld, 2007, p. 121). I encourage teachers to create such an open climate and welcome students' knowledge into the curriculum, enabling it to grow and emerge as a source of student pride. Below, I spotlight three such strategies that can be used during the problem identification phase of civic literacy projects to this end.

Independent Writing

The social justice writing assignment illustrates the value of organizing informal, independent writing activities that ask students to document their observations and insights about society, and their communities in particular. The project began when Scott Rosner asked his students to make ethnographic observations of their urban neighborhood and record them in writing. In turn, they collected "seed ideas" for their projects. Their lists and descriptions of seed ideas, which included social problems as well as change-making efforts, continued to grow throughout the problem identification phase. Therefore, their notebooks came to house a wealth of information to review when they ultimately self-selected the problems they would study and write about for the remainder of the term.

The strategy of independent writing as a generative starting point in the writing process is common in writing and reading workshop-style teaching. In this approach, students keep a record of "territories" that they would like to cover as writers (Atwell, 1998, p. 120). These territories include topics, purposes, audiences, and genres that interest them. More generally, in writer's notebooks, youth might write about their memories, what they overhear others talking about, or what surprises or angers them (Fletcher, 2010). Students continually add to their notebooks throughout the year and consult them when beginning a new piece. In a civic literacy project, students can use their territories and notebook entries to list and describe the social and political issues and events that matter to them, the people they want to contact to provoke change, and the messages they would communicate. They might also collect photographs and newspaper clippings that illustrate various social problems in their communities.

Like Scott's 8th-graders, Katherine Bomer's elementary-age students productively consulted their notebooks when beginning a project entitled "Writing for Social Action":

> Katherine's students began by finding previous notebook entries connected to politically important topics. They also wrote additional notebook entries as they looked at the world through lenses related to social justice. Then they shared their notebook entries with partners during class meetings every day. The kids' strong feelings about what they had written about in their notebooks led to lots of talk throughout the day. (Bomer & Bomer, 2001, p. 123)

As seen in this case, students' writing can drive their interest in civic life, promote classroom dialogue, and help students articulate their thoughts and stories about civic problems.

Open Forum

Problem identification can also happen primarily through oral dialogue. The 9th-graders in The Leadership Academy aired their concerns about the inadequacy of their sex education in such a way when their teachers organized an open forum to surface the students' concerns about their community. After one student complained that students did not know at what age to have sex, others shared related concerns. Therefore, the open forum showed not only the educators' interest in airing students' civic concerns but also the way such forums can help students acknowledge a common worry or cause.

A similar forum was enacted at the start of a social action project set in Cabrini-Green, Chicago, Illinois, in a school portrayed in *Spectacular Things Happen Along the Way* (Schultz, 2008). Brian Schultz, a 5th-grade teacher, asked the students to brainstorm problems that affected them and their community. After 89 were listed on the board, one student noted, "Most of the problems on that list have to do with our school building bein' messed up. Our school is a dump!" (p. 1). It suffered from the inadequacies that face other urban schools—the classrooms were cold, windows were cracked, and the students had neither an auditorium nor a lunchroom for use. Following the forum, the inadequacy of their school became the central problem of their year-long civic project during which Schultz's students created a sophisticated advocacy campaign calling on the district to build a new school.

Interestingly, Brian Schultz (2008) did not intentionally set out to engage the students in a deep form of social change. His primary goal, reiterated many times in the text, was to create a student-centered initiative.

More concerned with the process than any particular product, he wanted to give the students authority over the curriculum and address their emergent needs and interests. In turn, the 5th-grade students were positioned as active agents from the start of the project, as they determined their central focus during the first open forum.

"Take a Stand" Activities

Finally, it is helpful to get students up out of their seats and require them to air their thinking by moving. I call these "take a stand" activities, as they ask students to physically stand by other students or signs that represent their thoughts on social problems. This occurred in the park project when the students walked around the class to find other classmates who felt the same way about the budget cuts as they did. This activity served to make student thinking available as a source of knowledge for the class during the problem identification phase of the project.

The Beyond Today facilitators also enacted "take a stand" activities to prompt student thinking about racial segregation. For example, at the conclusion of an activity about Jim Crow and legally enforced segregation, a facilitator asked the students "Does segregation exist today?" The students were to show their opinion by standing on a line somewhere between the signs "Strongly Agree" and "Strongly Disagree." Of the 22 participating students, two students stood next to "Strongly Disagree," three students stood in the middle, and the rest stood next to "Strongly Agree," illustrating that the majority of the students could identify segregation as a current public matter. Such a polling activity can be used as an opportunity for students to introduce their views on a range of potential social problems. When one seems to ignite significant student interest—either because of agreement or disagreement—the class has identified a social problem to put at the heart of their civic literacy project.

Similarly, teachers can ask students to stand by signs that present different social problems, so as to show which problem interests or bothers them the most. For example, say a teacher knows that the students are concerned about the United States intervening in wars abroad, the prison system, and global warming. These topics were raised by many of the students the day before when the teacher asked students to list 10 problems facing their community and the country. To continue the process of problem identification, the teacher might write these terms down on three sheets of construction paper, post them in separate areas of the classroom, and ask students to stand by the one that they would most want to address in a civic literacy project. The students could then be invited to explain to another student standing by the sign their personal connections and thoughts about the topic. These students might end up working in coalitions to address problems related to their topics of choice.

CONCLUSION

There is much work to be done. Civic problems, existing in many forms, are waiting to be addressed. The problem identification phase of civic literacy projects is about naming these problems and selecting those that will be confronted. Ideally, this selection is done in a way that honors the students' life experiences and viewpoints. Whether through the use of independent writing, oral dialogue in an open forum, "take a stand" activities, or other methods, civic literacy projects are generatively ignited when students' civic concerns are surfaced. Youth have thoughts of how their society could be better. Therefore, it is fruitful for their voices to be made central in the process of problem identification.

CHAPTER 3

Problem Exploration

In civic literacy projects, problem identification, or the process of naming pressing social problems, is attached to problem exploration, the process wherein students build robust understandings of these problems. To foster problem exploration, teachers and students comprehend and critique information on their chosen problems using multiple resources. They examine print texts, including books and articles; visual and digital texts, including movies and photographs; and oral texts, including community interviews. As teachers support this phase of the project, they can see their students' sensitivities and awareness about the problems grow. Alternatively, teachers and students might identify a civic problem and take action around it without fully understanding how that problem impacts them and others. This is an unfortunate consequence of enacting short-term civic projects in which teachers do not structure time for sustained exploration of pressing civic problems. This chapter prepares teachers to avoid this possibility and instead use classroom time and resources to meaningfully build contextual knowledge about public issues.

I open the chapter with illustrations of how educators in two anchor cases (see Chapter 1 for their introductions) supported students to study civic problems. This leads into a rationale for why students benefit from developing contextual understandings of civic problems. Next, at the heart of the chapter, I review eight types of resources that can drive students' problem exploration. The chapter concludes with a look at a select number of learning strategies that students can use when working to comprehend and critique these resources.

CASES TO CONSIDER

The race awareness after-school program and the park project illustrate ways teachers and students can study civic problems. Through the phase of problem exploration, they consulted texts that could refine their views about racial discrimination and the park budget and help them meet unit goals regarding these problems. I present short discussions of both cases so to offer pictures of problem exploration in action.

Race Awareness After-School Program

To review, the race awareness after-school program was a year-long program directed by multiple facilitators employed by a nonprofit organization, Beyond Today. As presented in their mission statement, the program sought to bring together young students from de facto segregated neighborhoods to engage in a curriculum focused on discrimination, inequality, and social justice and to develop leadership towards social change.

In order to study forms of discrimination, the curriculum presented the topic on two levels: (1) discrimination as it has occurred in history and (2) contemporary examples of discrimination both inside and outside of the students' communities. For example, to learn about the historical Brown versus Board of Education decision, students perused a facilitator-created museum exhibit of primary documents related to the trial as they jotted their observations in journals. To learn about a contemporary instance of discrimination, students worked in small groups to read a testimony from a Somali American living in Portland, Maine, who was teased for her head covering. They presented the main idea to the other students through a skit. Then, in a whole group discussion, they considered the following questions: (1) "How does discrimination in the past compare to discrimination today?" (2) "What would you do if you witnessed discrimination today?" As illustrated in these discussion questions, the facilitators prompted the students to form connections between historical and contemporary examples of discrimination and consider their own personal responses (Epstein & Lipschultz, 2012).

To teach about discrimination in the past and today, the facilitators integrated a range of both visual and print texts. For example, two lessons entailed photo analysis, framing photographs as valuable visual resources. In one, the students were instructed to look at a picture of a café from the Jim Crow era with separate entrances labeled "White" and "Colored" and to have a "silent conversation" about it. This entailed silently writing and responding to their peers' thoughts on large poster-size papers. At the subsequent meeting, the facilitators presented pictures of a small, fragile building identified as a "Black School" and a big, sturdy building identified as a "White School," also from the Jim Crow era. The students were prompted, using a worksheet, to reflect on the differences between the structures.

The students also studied print texts. During one lesson on recent forms of de facto segregation, the students read an excerpt from Jonathan Kozol's *Amazing Grace* (1996) explaining people's inclination to stay in segregated groups. Kozol's first-person account discussed how after a certain stop on the public transit line, all of the passengers were Black. They also read a testimony from a White tourist visiting a historically Black neighborhood in their city. The tourist referenced some well-known historical sites as well as his acknowledgment of the stark segregation—he was the only White person for blocks. Additionally, the tourist claimed that he feared for his safety because of what he had seen on television. Indeed, mainstream media often portrays communities of color as exclusively crime ridden and places to be fearful of instead of also illustrating their strengths. The students were instructed to view these texts, and others, and discuss them together.

The Park Project

The park project was loosely directed by two overarching objectives: The students will be able to (1) deliberate and express opinions on the budget deficit and (2) generate persuasive essays on budget cuts to a local park. These objectives reflected the teachers' dedication to addressing students' literacy skills. They intended to embed a persuasive writing assignment as well as oral literacy tasks, such as deliberation, into the project.

In order to both argue something persuasively in writing and deliberate about it through speaking, the students needed to build knowledge about the issue at hand. Towards this end, they focused on print, digital, and oral texts. For their print texts, they read newspaper articles and a public statement from the state governor explaining the necessity of the budget cuts. The students worked through the texts in small reading groups and were instructed to take notes on their findings.

Then, the students learned about the perspectives of key people involved in the legislative struggle around the state budget. For example, as the students began drafting their letters in protest of the budget cuts, Deanne Holly, their English and social studies teacher, directed them to the website of their local assemblyperson to learn about his concerns and then infer his stance on the cuts to the park budget. She modeled how to find information on the website that they could use to understand his position on the park budget. For example, they found a section where he represented himself as an advocate for youth and as skilled in leveraging limited resources. These details and others led the students to believe that their assemblyperson would be in favor of restoring the park budget.

Finally, they enacted a deliberative forum to air the students' knowledge on possible ways to ensure full funding to the park. This was a key oral literacy experience as it asked the students to speak their views and listen to those of classmates. Through the discussion, the students proposed that the park raise service fees, open a souvenir center to create revenue, and hold a benefit concert or basketball game. Students also proposed the benefits and challenges associated with each approach during the whole-class discussion while Deanne recorded their ideas on the board. The deliberation offered them opportunities to articulate particular values that seemed to influence their understanding of the issue. For example, some students were interested in the social capital of the park. They thought that the souvenir shop would attract more tourists and the benefit concert would bring "fans" and "exposure" to the issue. Others were concerned about the economic status of community members. They feared that with added fees, the park would become too expensive for people. As a result of the deliberation, students could bring their own knowledge into the class as oral texts to explore with their peers. Ultimately, they each chose particular proposals for filling the budget gap to share with the assemblyperson in letters.

The race awareness after-school program as well as the park project integrated multiple sources of information, including photographs, newspaper articles, and student knowledge shared orally. In turn, the cases illustrate how teachers and students can consult various types of resources and utilize reading, writing, and speaking/listening skills so as to fully explore civic problems. These cases will be referenced throughout the chapter, as I revisit the use of the resources and teaching strategies discussed above as well as introduce additional resources and strategies that proved valuable during the projects.

BUILDING CONTEXT

Students' efforts to study a particular civic problem serve an important goal—to build their contextual understanding of that problem. Such contextual understandings are developed when students look at multiple texts and think critically about how each text presents the problem as it exists now, in the past, and for different groups of citizens. Through this process, civic problems can be seen as related to political, social, and economic systems, and the complexity of the problems emerges. Low-income students of color in Los Angeles built such contextual knowledge when they studied the tracking practices in their school that resulted in their placement in "regular" (as opposed to "honors") classes that would not prepare them for 4-year college attendance (Oakes & Rogers, 2006). Analyzing empirical, theoretical, and autobiographical data, they formed a "nuanced understanding of why their struggle was something more complex and daunting than simply learning the steps or protocols one might find in a self-help pamphlet" (Oakes & Rogers, 2006, p. 54). In this model, students grapple with information and sharpen their explanations of pressing, public problems.

Specifically, as students build contextual knowledge, they (1) form a historical framework around the identified problem and (2) recognize the viewpoints of multiple stakeholders in regard to addressing it. The discussion below highlights these two aspects of problem exploration.

Building a Historical Framework

One way for students to build a contextual understanding of a social problem is to recognize how it has been situated throughout history. Through this work, students acknowledge that their selected problem is not fully isolated and unique and instead has manifested in different forms throughout generations. For example, students advocating for immigration reform should understand how immigrants of different decades faced discrimination and how they organized to protect their rights.

Such a historical framework can serve many purposes. First, in giving students the opportunity to examine social problems in history and how they exist in contemporary times, students can see that they are not alone and that they can relate to and possibly find support from the stories of individuals from the past. With this "identity support" students can see how their own experiences reflect the struggles of others and gain the impetus to work as activists (Lewis-Charp, Yu, & Soukamneuth, 2006, p. 27). And, as students draw from history to make sense of their experiences, they can recognize that there is a social use to studying the past (Barton & Levstik, 1998; VanSledright, 2002). Finally, acknowledgment of historical schemas builds an understanding of the deep-rootedness of social problems and citizens' responses to these problems. For example, students might become aware of labor organizing when a strike occurs in their hometown. Using this instance as an opening for continued problem exploration, they could learn about the history of advocacy for collective bargaining rights. This could inform them that any one dispute over workers' rights is not a passing fad; it represents a long-term historical trend.

As educators teach students how to acknowledge broad social systems and trends of inequity, their efforts can be seen in relation to critical theory. Critical theorists base their work on a concern for systemic, historical trends of power and privilege (Fletcher, 2000). From such a critical gaze, citizens work with the assumption that "all thought is fundamentally mediated by power relations that are social and historically constituted" (Kincheloe & McLaren, 2003, p. 452). Here, individuals are not exclusively free agents, but instead, their actions and beliefs reflect social and historical patterns. Teachers can structure ways to explore these patterns with youth.

In studying the historical roots of social issues, students can meet some role models. For example, if addressing questions of how to fully integrate

LGBTQ students into a school community, students might explore the often hidden history of LGBTQ achievements:

> Texts that teachers select can serve to communicate to all of their students that there are and have been positive and powerful people in the world who experience same-sex attraction and/or gender variance, such as Langston Hughes, Gertrude Stein, Alice Walker, and Oscar Wilde, among many others. (Blackburn, 2012, p. 40)

This learning can help students critique trends of homophobic bullying in their school and advocate for curricula that include LGBTQ achievements as possible action steps.

The race awareness after-school program serves as another example of a program that sought to develop students' historical understanding of a social issue—segregation. Specifically, students studied historical incidents of racial segregation and discrimination from the Jim Crow era as well as cases of local, present segregation. This curriculum forwarded the idea that the discrimination in their city was not unique or short-term; it reflected a lasting historical circumstance.

Building students' historical understandings is a challenging task. In particular, some students look at historical examples of injustice and dismiss them as having happened "back then." For example, in Seixas's (1994) work, 10th-grade students argued that racism in society has decreased over time and that we continue to move "towards a moral end" (p. 296). They struggled to see the ways that racism affected the lives of citizens in their time.

Given this, educators productively link historical examples of social problems to contemporary examples, ideally focusing on those influencing the students' personal lives (Epstein & Lipschultz, 2012). For example, if students are studying the questions of whether and how a military draft should be exercised, they can first air their own experiences with and knowledge about military recruitment. Students might have family members in the military and can tell stories about how they got involved, or students might discuss their experiences being approached by military recruiters. After airing their own experiences, they can study how citizens have been enlisted in or recruited for the military in the past, focusing possibly on the Vietnam War and World War II. This could then generatively lead into a comparative study where students analyze how people get involved in the military today versus in the past, identifying the benefits and drawbacks to a draft. When building historical awareness during a civic literacy project, the connectedness between yesterday and today should remain clear so that students critically analyze what is currently happening around them in light of historical precedents.

Analyzing Multiple Stakeholders' Viewpoints

Students also build contextual knowledge of a social problem when they name and deliberate on diverse viewpoints that exist in regard to any one social problem. Specifically, deliberation is most effective when it provides a space for potentially competing perspectives and their benefits and drawbacks. Parker (2003) argues that in deliberative forums, it is important to air the diverse opinions of all stakeholders. Towards this end, he explains how students can create a "map" of the perspectives on how a civic problem should be addressed, and that this map should illustrate the problem's nuance and complexity (p. 116). Then, using the map, teachers can structure deliberative forums in which alternatives to civic problems are weighed, and a path of action is ultimately chosen.

This type of teaching yields many benefits. First, engaging with multiple perspectives through a deliberative process enables students to understand how to work productively in public spaces (Parker, 1997). Whether teachers believe that citizens commonly deliberate or that they *should* do so more, they can teach their students how to acknowledge, analyze, and deliberate on competing perspectives so as to democratically engage with social issues (Hess, 2009b). Through deliberation, students learn to complicate or question their original perspectives and gain confidence to engage with others on public matters.

Second, teachers can display multiple opinions on an issue so as to ignite students' curiosity about the issue and best prepare them for civic action. For example, high school social studies teachers reported that teaching about the federal budget, national debt, and budget deficits—critical civic topics—would be controversial and therefore would spur student interest (Marri et al., 2012). Then, when students learn and dialogue about the competing public policy perspectives and issues related to these topics, developing deep understandings, "students will be empowered to demand capable leadership and effective solutions to fiscal challenges from public officials" (p. 209). As students explore multiple perspectives on an issue, they build their readiness to develop their own arguments and counterarguments and advocate for particular policy changes.

Third, through students' examination of multiple perspectives, they can use critical literacy skills, enabling them to highlight the complexities of problems as opposed to viewing them from an essentialist perspective (McLaughlin & DeVoogd, 2004). To this end, teachers use "juxtaposing" as a technique and integrate texts that express different perspectives on a social problem—including texts from different genres such as photos, videos, and lyrics (McLaughlin & DeVoogd, 2004, p. 58).

During the park project, the teachers integrated texts that portrayed multiple perspectives on the park budget deficit. For example, they distrib-uted a letter from the state governor explaining the necessity of the budget cuts. They also read newspaper articles that explained problems with the cuts, quoting from advocates who claimed the importance of parks for pub-lic health and the economy. One article stated that even during the Great Depression, the government did not close parks. This resonated with a stu-dent who raised it during class discussion as important. Indeed, this fact illustrated that public officials from the past have made different decisions than the current governor. Through this research, the students could learn that public policy solutions are debated and that individuals with power advocate for different options.

As teachers consider the range of viewpoints to introduce on any one issue, they will encounter questions about the extent to which they should frame an issue as controversial and how many different perspectives on that issue they want to validate (Hess, 2005). Some teachers might deny that an issue is controversial, seeing it as "closed," and present perspectives that represent one side of a public debate. Others might present what they see as a "balanced" set of views on an issue that they see as controversial. Yet those who don't believe that issue is controversial would see a teacher's presented set of views as biased because it includes a perspective that they believe is not valid. This is a complicated enterprise, further explored in Chapter 5.

A primary strategy that teachers can use to work with this complica-tion is to publicly air their thoughts on how they will present controver-sial issues and deliberate on these decisions with colleagues (Hess, 2007). Teachers might sit down with their coworkers to explore which viewpoints they should surface about the fiscal deficit, marriage equality, U.S. interven-tions in wars abroad, and a host of other conversations that may be seen as controversial. I have also had generative experiences talking with those involved in advocacy around a political issue. These individuals helped me understand the different viewpoints that most commonly define public dia-logue on an issue. In these conversations, activists and community organiz-ers explained their perspectives as well as their opponents' perspectives, and allowed me to consider a range of viewpoints to address in the curriculum. Working with others on how to present and explore multiple perspectives and policy alternatives on civic issues is an important step to take when deciding how to frame the phase of problem exploration.

By building a historical framework and analyzing multiple stakehold-ers' perspectives, students can deeply explore civic problems, not taking them for granted or settling for simplistic solutions. Teachers and students draw on a broad range of materials so as to support this process. The next section of this chapter reviews some of the options.

RESOURCES TO BUILD CONTEXTUAL
UNDERSTANDINGS OF CIVIC PROBLEMS

The following list of resources is informed by the idea that learning best occurs when multiple modalities are engaged. This means that oral, print, and visual texts should be used to engage students as they explore a civic problem at hand. If only one type of text is incorporated, then students who prefer learning through a different modality will be denied opportunities to fully develop their views on the problem. Curricula that are relevant and multimodal prompt and support multiple forms of student participation (Schultz, 2009), and robust student participation is strongly desired in civic literacy projects. With this motivation, teachers and students consult a range of resources, such as those below, so as to get to know their identified problem in all its complexity.

Journalism

Newspaper and magazine articles as well as radio broadcasts and online journalism might be a first stop for teachers and students who are looking to understand a civic problem. This is particularly the case if the issue is timely and getting attention in the media. Not only is the information current, but adolescents' discussions of the news with parents and friends predict higher levels of civic engagement now and in the future (Erentaite, Zukauskiene, Beyers, & Pilkauskaite-Valickiene, 2012). Furthermore, when teachers require the use of news media in class, their students are more likely to have favorable attitudes towards the First Amendment and free speech activities (Lopez, Levine, Dautrich, & Yalof, 2009). For these reasons, teachers prioritize the discussion of journalism in civic education projects.

Use of the Internet enables teachers to readily access media sources. While teachers might arrange for some periodicals to be delivered to the classroom, other pieces of journalism might be accessed online. Then, many articles on the Internet immediately link to other "related" articles. So, in a short period of time, students can access a variety of viewpoints and learn of multiple stories related to their identified civic problem.

For example, a class might take up the issue of gun control public policy. If there was a tragic shooting, newspapers would likely print articles covering residents' perspectives, explaining the politics of how politicians have voted on gun-control legislation, and comparing the stances of different advocacy organizations on the issue. Given the timeliness of media resources as well as their accessibility on the Internet, such texts play a valuable role in informing students' civic understandings.

One challenge that can emerge with journalism is that the pieces might not be on the students' reading levels. Teachers might be enthusiastic to bring in up-to-date reporting on an identified civic problem, but the writing could pose challenges for the students. For example, in the park project, the teachers used newspaper articles to build students' understandings of the state budget and why multiple groups were advocating for limited funds to be used in different ways. Yet, the teachers noted that the texts were at a reading level that tested the students' skills, especially those of the English language learners. Specifically, one of the teachers expressed concern that the students would struggle with the vocabulary. The teachers therefore created a word wall exclusively for the park project, and when reading aloud the articles, they would think aloud their explanations of particular vocabulary words. The word wall included the following terms and their definitions: fiscal, deficit, advocacy, jeopardize, unprecedented, exacerbating, diminished. With such reading supports, students' reading proficiencies can build. The teachers used a high interest, meaningful way to learn vocabulary and work with texts that were beyond their students' independent reading level.

Another key challenge that emerges with journalism, particularly web-based journalism, is related to the reliability of the sources. As students surf the web, they might encounter sources (i.e., blogs and personal webpages) that represent biased viewpoints. This serves as another reason to reflect on the importance of teaching students to seek out multiple viewpoints and cultivate an appetite for a diversity of perspectives. Yet, before such a diversity of perspectives is found and digested by the students, exposure to any one extreme view can be problematic. Given the fact that anyone can publish anything on the Internet and the way that a person's stance can profoundly distort the information they are presenting, teachers must "help students become 'healthy skeptics' about the accuracy of the information they encounter" (Leu, 1997, p. 65). While this critical stance has value for all texts students read, teachers should be particularly mindful about teaching it when reading the Internet.

Additionally, teachers support students by creating clear search guidelines and providing lists of websites to visit (Sutherland-Smith, 2002). By taking these steps, teachers better ensure that students will work with a focused set of on-topic and reliable sources. In particular, when teachers direct students to a series of preselected websites, they can ensure that the students are exposed to different, yet justified viewpoints on civic issues.

Other Nonfiction Informational Texts

Other nonfiction print texts, aside from journalism, present information that helps students build contextual understandings of public matters. First, particular books enable students to understand discrete civic topics. For example, *Immigration: The Ultimate Teen Guide* (Kleyn, 2011) is a nonfiction text written for a teen audience and covers both historical and contemporary issues around immigration.

Second, students might locate statistical data related to a civic topic. Continuing the example of immigration, students could research information on how rates of immigration have changed over the decades. In the race awareness after-school program, the students studied statistics on the racial demographics of the different neighborhoods in their city, information that can be found on government and census websites.

Third, nonfiction texts that present a variety of viewpoints on social issues are valuable as they build students' understandings of the competing ideas expressed about their chosen social problem. The Choices Program (see www.choices.edu) provides resources that outline various policy options to critical civic issues. For example, they published a lesson entitled "Debating the U.S. Response to Syria" (2013) that includes four clearly written passages, each on a different possible response. The National Issues Forums Institute (NIFI) also offers issue books that outline multiple stances on current civic issues. Each issue book presents three to four approaches on national issues, including those related to social security, government regulation of the Internet, and violence among youth. These materials strongly promote deliberation in schools, as they clearly outline each approach as well as its benefits and drawbacks, presenting students with the content knowledge necessary to engage in the public debate about the issue.

Fourth, students should study texts on the history of an issue that they are taking up or the impact, in general, of movements for social change. Such stories will illustrate for the students how their civic literacy projects are not isolated events but connected to a history of groups naming social problems and organizing to address them. For example, *A Different Mirror: A History of Multicultural America* (Takaki, 1993) tells the compelling story of the labor struggles in the garment industry between 1909 and 1920. As a result of strikes and other campaigns, the largely Jewish American campaign won a 50-hour work week, salary increases, and preferential hiring of workers who were union members; the industry went from a largely unorganized enterprise to an industry where workers were protected. Takaki details many examples of how racially and ethnically diverse groups have organized for change, examples that can help students understand the historical traditions of advocacy and agitation.

A People's History of the United States (Zinn, 2003) and *Lies My Teacher Told Me: Everything Your American History Textbook Got Wrong* (Loewen, 2007) are also known for the way they integrate frequently unnamed injustices and victories for justice in U.S. history often absent in traditional textbooks. For primary sources, *Voices of a People's History of the United States* (Zinn & Arnove, 2004) exposes voices of individuals from American history who have advocated for change, such as Frederick Douglass and Emma Goldman, bringing to light their struggles and campaigns.

Finally, students can study Supreme Court cases to understand competing perspectives on social issues that have immediate contemporary relevance and that are controversial (Hess & Marri, 2002). Students can read the briefs from both sides of a case as well as the judges' opinions so as to engage in their own deliberation on the proper decision. For some schools where teaching controversial issues is frowned upon, teaching Supreme Court cases is a way to get a relevant, controversial issue into the curriculum. For example, by studying Roe versus Wade, students could have their first school-sanctioned conversation about abortion. Students might even study Supreme Court cases as they are unfolding in their time. In Spring 2012, the case on the constitutionality of the Affordable Care Act gained much media attention and might have been placed at the center of a civic literacy project on health care. Supreme Court cases illustrate the desire for citizens to both work together and recognize their different interests, and therefore a study of them can present models for how students should engage in their own deliberations on issues that are important to them (Parker, 1997).

Many nonfiction texts quickly become outdated. The National Issues Forums Institute (NIFI) readily prints new issue books to stay up to date, as the "hot" controversial topics for the country change and shift. The public policy proposals articulated to address any one civic concern also evolve. The use of an issue book on military intervention, for example, printed before the United States' strikes on Iraq and Afghanistan might seem inappropriate for use today. Therefore, when using "dated" nonfiction texts or primary sources, it is important for teachers to scaffold instruction that helps students recognize the authors' historical contexts. They can then turn the conversation to one in which they look at the historical trajectory of a perennial issue or debate. Additionally, teachers should seek out texts that discuss current iterations of social problems to study alongside the historical texts.

Narratives

Throughout human history, people have learned about the world through stories. Indeed, stories are particularly democratic sources of knowledge, as individuals learn from them without wealth, status, or formal education (Bell, 2010). Furthermore, a narrative allows the reader to relate to those in the story and view the context of characters' experiences with all the descriptive language that is common in these texts. To meet such characters, students read novels, memoirs, autobiographies, biographies, picture books, and digital stories—all texts that play valuable roles in civic literacy projects.

Specifically, teachers can prioritize literature that tells stories of people collaborating, working for the greater good of the community, and using agency in light of critical reflection—key aspects of activism (Simon & Norton, 2011). They can highlight transformative stories that portray the pursuit of social justice and challenges to the status quo (Banks, 1993; Bell, 2010). Such narrative texts present opportunities for students to analyze how characters get involved in civic pursuits, how they are shaped by their activism, and how they impact their communities.

Narrative texts also inspire students towards actions of their own, as they can be catalyzing forces for youth:

> Students can connect issues in almost any text they read to problems in their community and institutional or civic groups working to address them. Students reading Steinbeck's *Of Mice and Men* (1982) or Thomas Rivera's *And the Earth Did Not Devour Him* (2007) might engage in service-learning related to mi-grant workers. Students reading *The Taming of the Shrew* or Laurie Anderson's youth adult novel *Speak* might learn about and work with women's shelters, ho-tlines, and YWCA programs supporting survivors of abuse or sexual violence. (Beach et al., 2012, p. 64)

Here, four narrative texts are associated with real problems in the com-munity, and the authors claim that service-learning, a form of civic action explored in Chapter 4, can follow students' reading. The quote also sug-gests how pairings of narrative texts can build contextual understandings of issues, illustrating how different groups of people have been addressing similar injustices at different places and times in history. In particular, despite the fact that *The Taming of the Shrew* (Shakespeare, 1992) is a Shakespearean text while *Speak* (Anderson, 1999) illustrates a high school in modern times, the texts can be linked within a civic literacy project on abuse of women.

In the park project, the 7th-graders read *The Streets Are Free* (Kurusa, 1981)—a picture book that tells the story of a group of kids advocating for the building of a playground, ultimately in collaboration with other adult community members. It is based on a true story that happened in Venezuela. At the start of the story, their barrio contained no suitable place for the children to play, and the community members worked together to garner attention for the playground and later build it. Deanne Holly, the teacher directing the reading activity, prompted the students to form connections between the children in the story and their own work in reference to the local park. She raised questions about the overarching issues that motivated both projects, including, "When you live in a crowded area, you want to experience 'green spaces' and not have to go miles and miles to have green. Why might you want to live in a place that is green?" Both she and the cooperating special education teacher were pleased with the integration of this text, particularly because they saw it as comprehensible for the struggling readers in the class. It is ripe with visual cues as each page has a picture, and it is written with accessible vocabulary.

Teachers will likely face a challenge of finding texts that deal directly with the civic issues at hand if dedicated to the integration of narrative texts in civic literacy projects. This is particularly the case if the identified civic problem is very specific to one particular community. Given this, teachers might consider introducing a narrative text at the beginning of a civic literacy project so as to illustrate how characters in the story have dealt with a related issue or engaged in social change in general. This can inspire students to see the value of civic engagement. Then students can further explore their specific issue by consulting other texts.

Poetry and Song

Poems and songs are closely related because of the way that both texts are commonly read aloud, emphasizing oral expression as a key component of literacy. Students may be drawn to these texts because of their interest in speaking and listening and because of the ways poems and songs can describe social problems in meaningful and personal ways. Indeed, poetic texts read aloud, such as spoken word poetry or even more specifically hip-hop music, might encourage young people to listen closely to texts, appreciate their language and words, and get inspired to become wordsmiths on their own (Fisher, 2005). Finally, poems and songs are generally shorter than narrative stories contained in chapter books and can serve as user-friendly resources in civic literacy projects.

Songs and poems peppered the race awareness after-school curriculum. During one meeting, the Beyond Today facilitators enacted a lesson on *The Ballad of Eddie Klepp* (Brodsky, 1996), a song commemorating the first White man to play baseball in the Negro Leagues in 1946. The song names the historical context of the time—post–World War II, during the reign of the Jim Crow laws—and then gives a descriptive account of what it was like for Klepp to cross the color line. After studying the song and also Jackie Robinson's experience entering an all-White baseball league, the students identified similarities and differences in the ways Jackie Robinson and Eddie Klepp challenged racial boundaries. This song, studied alongside the story of Jackie Robinson, can help students recognize that people of all races cross racial lines and, in turn, contribute to a process of social change. Such a comparison of Klepp and Robinson can also lead students to reflect on forms of White privilege and the differences between activism of individuals or groups with disparate levels of power in society. Finally, if students are studying the racial segregation of their neighborhood, this song fosters

their historical knowledge of how segregation has manifested and been challenged in the past. In the after-school program, the students listened to it
while they read the printed lyrics—accessing two modalities simultaneously.

The race awareness after-school program also made use of poetry. In
one lesson, students worked in small groups to read "Merry-Go-Round"
by Langston Hughes (1994) and "Waiting at the Railroad Cafe" by Janet
Wong (1994)—two poems portraying segregation and racial discrimination from two different times in history. In "Merry Go-Round" the speaker
questions where the White and Colored sections of the merry-go-round are
because he is assuming that Jim Crow laws are being upheld. In "Waiting
at the Railroad Cafe" the speaker recalls an incident that occurred in the
mid-1970s when she and her father—both Asian—were not served and then
yelled at in a restaurant. After reading the poems, the associated lesson plan
prompted facilitators to ask, "What did the kids in each piece have in common? What was different? How does discrimination in the past compare
to discrimination today?" among other questions. Such questioning helps
students develop a historical context for the problem of racial segregation
and discrimination today.

Hip-hop might have played an additionally valuable role in the after-school program. It is a medium that often speaks personally to youth
growing up in urban environments, as the texts can directly describe their
experiences (Flores-Gonzalez, Rodriguez, & Rodriguez-Muniz, 2006). As
they listen to hip-hop, these young people can connect with each other and
realize that "their experiences are part of larger social issues plaguing their
community" (p. 187), building their contextual understandings of social
problems. In general, hip-hop is praised for the way it promotes social critique. As one teenager put it, "Hip hop makes me think and question things
going on around me" (Hallman, 2009, p. 43). For these reasons, teachers
look for opportunities to integrate hip-hop during the problem exploration
phase of civic literacy projects.

Furthermore, students can use hip-hop as a frame for sharing their own
experiences with social questions or problems. In a high school for pregnant teenagers, two students used hip-hop texts as models for their own
personal statements about pregnancy (Hallman, 2009). In these statements,
they communicated their desires to be agents and empowered in their lives.
Students' encounters with hip-hop help them not only build their contextual
understandings of social problems but also present them with models to use
as they craft their own statements about social problems.

Similar to narrative texts, it might be a challenge for teachers to find
poems and songs that are related to the civic issue that they are addressing
in their civic literacy project. Or, if a text is found, it might not provide sufficient detail to understand the complexity of the social problem at hand. To
address these challenges, poems and songs should be integrated into civic

literacy projects during the phase of problem exploration with other texts. If selected poems and songs are tangentially related to the identified problem, teachers can then integrate additional texts around them so as to scaffold opportunities for students to develop knowledge that is more closely related to the problem at hand.

Film, Television, and Other Visual Texts

Visual texts—television, photographs, films, and other nonprint images found in magazines, murals, and so forth—are powerful largely because of their accessibility. While print texts can put up roadblocks in reference to students' language skills, visual texts present as friendly entry points to students' studies. Furthermore, when teachers integrate visual texts, they validate the types of visual literacy experiences that are common for their students. It is arguable that citizens learn the majority of their knowledge about political processes and issues through visual media, such as television, yet this source of information is not used enough in civics curricula (Kubey, 2004).

The race awareness program championed itself on its ability to provide multiple entry points, and, in turn, the facilitators routinely presented students with visual texts along with other print and oral texts. For example, during the same lesson where students read an excerpt from Jonathan Kozol's *Amazing Grace* (1996), they also studied a map of their city, color coded to show the racial demographics of different areas, further confirming the racial segregation that Kozol references. And the students learned about the Jim Crow era both through the words of Langston Hughes and through photographs of the time. The visual texts helped ensure that the curriculum was accessible for all the students.

As films also powerfully illustrate civic problems, a valuable resource is *Teaching Social Issues with Film* (Russell, 2009). This text categorizes 180 films—biographies, documentaries, comedies, dramas, and so forth—related to 30 civic topics, including gang culture, abortion, and capital punishment. Teachers could readily turn to this text to select a film that addresses the civic issue at the heart of their project.

Indeed, films present a number of pedagogical possibilities for civic literacy projects. First, films enable students to connect with a character with great empathy—largely because they offer the same type of descriptive detail that is found in print narratives—and, in viewing them, youth might better understand the social problem the character faces. Second, the use of film might be particularly valuable if the teacher intends for the students to connect to a time in the past. As noted above, documents that represent historical times can tell stories that are dismissed as having happened "back then," yet when viewed through a film, any one historical incident can seem more present and alive, enabling students to make stronger connections to the time portrayed.

Illustrating the power of integrating film into a civic literacy project, if students are studying questions about disability, or mental illness, they might view *A Beautiful Mind* (Grazer & Howard, 2001). This text presents a compassionate and inspiring view of a man suffering from mental illness who is ultimately respected for his intelligence and achievements as a mathematician. Following a viewing of the film, teachers can prompt students to question how people with disabilities are generally treated in society and how schools, workplaces, and public spaces in general could better welcome and affirm the experiences of people with disabilities. Students can also explore how people with disabilities are portrayed in other media such as television and advertisements, leading them to develop media literacy skills and, potentially, a desire to advocate for more just representations of disability.

One unique challenge that can emerge with the use of film and other visual texts is that they are often introduced in classrooms as a "treat." Both teachers and students can feel that their viewing of a film is "time off," and they do not engage in the same critical analysis that they might if they were reading a print text. In particular, if teachers avoid prompting the students to question the films, the students are denied opportunities to express their analysis of them. While students should critically analyze visual texts and recognize how persuasion and propaganda function in media such as television, these skills are routinely not prioritized in education (Kubey, 2004).

To avoid this, teachers can prepare a set of "think-alouds"—where they talk out loud their comprehension and critique of the visual texts—and guided focus questions for the students' use with the texts. These exercises are rather normative with print texts and should be extended to visual texts. Specifically, teachers might stop movies at different points during the viewing so as to prompt the students to consider how a civic problem is being portrayed, to what extent they agree or disagree with the portrayal, and how the historical context of the film compares to the students' lived political realities.

Community-Specific Information

When students meaningfully utilize community-based resources in their problem exploration, they learn how local community members address or experience social problems. Students gain such knowledge of their community by conducting interviews of community members or collecting and studying surveys documenting community-based issues, among other strategies. If civic engagement entails connecting with others towards a strong democracy (Barber, 2003), then it is essential that a process be put in place that helps students learn about the viewpoints of those most immediately around them. Furthermore, in accessing such viewpoints, students are given opportunities to place the more official knowledge that they might find in textbooks or other mass-produced texts in comparison to the knowledge manifested in their local contexts (Apple, 2000).

The teachers in the park project recognized the importance of such texts. The year before the park project, they enacted a civic literacy project on the potential expansion of a nearby university into their neighborhood. To learn about community viewpoints on the expansion, the students went to different locations, such as restaurants, and asked residents their opinions. The teachers identified this as a very "authentic" learning opportunity. While some community members chose not to speak to the students, others shared colorful viewpoints on the benefits and obstacles that the expansion might bring, presenting multiple perspectives on the issue at hand.

Or, instead of leaving the school, students can invite community members into the classroom and interview them. The pedagogy around classroom interviews is fully explored in *Classroom Interviews: A World of Learning* (Rogovin, 1998). Rogovin, an elementary school teacher, regularly makes space for interviews with community members during thematic units on topics including "Our school neighborhood," "Native American history and culture" and "People at work" (Rogovin, 1998, pp. 26–27). The students display their prior knowledge on the topic at the start of the interview. Then, they ask questions and record the information they learn during the interview and use it to write after the interview. The interviews have also informed the class's social action efforts. For example, in the "People at work" unit, the students learned about child labor during their interview of a woman who had been a child laborer in Mexico. They drew on this interview when writing a play on child labor and sweatshop conditions that was performed for the families of the students, influencing the audience to think about these issues and advocate for just protections for workers.

Conducting community interviews is an engaging assignment for older students as well. Students might compose oral histories of community members to learn about how a social issue shaped their town or school in previous years. When a group of high school students conducted oral histories on community members' experiences growing up in Los Angeles, they identified how they were not alone in their struggle for racial equality (Oakes & Rogers, 2006).

Students can also gather community-based information on social problems by collecting data on their communities through observations and surveys. In one civic project, introduced in Chapter 2, teenagers solicited and collected hundreds of complaint forms from students in local junior and high schools (Kwon, 2008). In studying the forms, the youth learned of their peers' concerns with their teachers' grading, school bathroom accessibility, and other issues. Alternatively, gathering and analyzing information from the community might entail giving students clipboards and a series of focus questions and asking them to record data on a series of potential public matters such as the parks, crosswalks, homeless shelters, and public transportation in their community. Or students can use digital video or audio equipment to document the conditions of their neighborhoods and schools (Duncan-Andrade, 2006). They might interview individuals in their community, record events on video cameras, or take pictures of buildings, trash collection, or conditions in their schools—just a few possible areas of focus.

A key challenge that emerges with this type of data is in regard to permissions. While students might readily embrace the exciting possibility of learning from a broad range of community members, any one local community member might not be interested in sharing stories. Alternatively, community members might want to share but express concern about how their stories or thoughts are going to be later represented by the students. Youth seeking out community-based knowledge should be prepared for these possibilities and take preparatory steps to lessen community members' concerns. First, teachers and students should seek out approval from school administrators to engage community members and then report to those being interviewed and surveyed that the project has this support and that they represent the school. Second, students can compose a consent form for community members to sign, ensuring the people they speak to or survey that their names will be replaced by pseudonyms, or fake names, if they wish. Other community members might be proud to be associated with what they say and might encourage the students to use their names in their writing.

"Expert" Resources

While lay community members are able to share their personal and often historically rooted views on an issue, others work professionally on an issue and know about it in a particularly informed way. These professionals might be office holders, representatives of nonprofit organizations, or lobbyists. When learning from these "expert" resource people, students are exposed to up-to-date knowledge about the nature of an issue or how it is being addressed.

Ideally, resource people are integrated into the classroom in focused ways. In these cases, a local governmental representative or community organizer does not give a speech on his or her stance on a range of issues but instead comes in prepared to talk about the specific issue the students are studying (Hess, 2004). The resource person might first answer the students' questions on the issue, then circulate among the students as they analyze different stances on it, and finally moderate a discussion about it. The resource person might even "chair" a simulated city-council hearing or an organizational board meeting on the topic.

When the 9th-graders involved in the safe sex health project decided that they wanted to bring needed information to their school about safe sex practices, they invited professionals that focus on this issue to share their "expert" knowledge. At the start of the fair, all the 9th-graders gathered in the auditorium for a presentation from a professor of public health on whom they should turn to with their questions about sex. This immediately centered the knowledge of an outside expert. Then, the students walked around a series of tables, and representatives from various nonprofit organizations passed out materials and spoke with the students. The distributed brochures addressed topics including emergency birth control, body image, male self-exams for sexually transmitted diseases, AIDS/HIV, and teenagers' health care rights (e.g., teens can get the results of an HIV test without their parents' knowing). Then, after lunch, the visiting nonprofit representatives ran sessions on these issues. While the students organizing the fair enacted it as an action step, this action step enabled the students attending the fair to explore issues about sexual health by learning from individuals and organizations that were particularly prepared and knowledgeable in this area. If students cannot attend a fair or workshops led by representatives from nonprofit organizations, as was the case during the health fair, students can study the stances and knowledge of such organizations by reading from their websites.

The park project was also enhanced with the knowledge of such "expert" resources. In particular, the 7th-grade students met with a representative of the parks department for their city. She eagerly came to their classroom and framed the problem of the slashed funds to the park. First, she reviewed the role of the governor and the legislature and explained how they determine how much tax money gets sent to different agencies (e.g., education, shelters, transportation, parks). Then, she explained how the money that goes to the parks department gets used. This helped the students understand why the outdoor pool in their local park, for example, might have been closed if more money was not allocated for the parks. Finally, she encouraged the students to get active on the issue. She reminded them that the budget had not yet been confirmed and that they should express their opinions about how money should get spent. She was compelling, commenting that "this is the moment" for action and proclaiming, "Your letters can make a difference!" Student questions were addressed throughout the presentation, and the students took notes on ideas that they thought they might want to include in their letters to their local assemblyperson.

When utilizing resource people in a civic literacy project, it is important that students recognize that they need not adopt the stance of any one person in its entirety. Students might feel that the resource people are the sole "experts," and therefore their views are fully correct. Yes, they are "experts" in the sense that they know a lot about the issue and have determined a particular stance on it based on their professional work in the area. However, as with any text, classroom instruction can support students to use critical reading and listening skills with which they question how or why the articulated views are partial. This process is ignited when the views of resource people are placed in comparison to the views of others, especially if the issue being addressed is controversial and the resource people do not portray it as such. Ideally, the resource people are not framed as unquestionable authorities, but instead students are given opportunities to come into conversation with them and their ideas.

Student Views

As students learn about social problems, it is often generative for them to study their own and their peers' experiences with the problems. Linda Christensen, a high school English teacher, presents pedagogical ideas in *Teaching for Joy and Justice* (2009) that offer models for this. In one project Christensen details, her students wrote personal narratives telling stories of incidents of injustice from their lives. These included stories in which the students were targets, allies, perpetrators, and bystanders—terms the students explored as a whole class before they wrote their narratives. In one story, for example, a student spoke of his experience living in a house affected by domestic violence.

After the class heard their peers' stories in what she calls a "read-around," Christensen prompted them to answer reflection questions by citing specific examples from the stories:

> How do people feel when they are the targets of injustice? When they are laughed at? Excluded? How do they feel when they gather the courage to stand up for someone else, when they fight back against ignorance and hate? Why didn't some of us act even when we felt immoral standing by as a witness to injustice? (p. 89)

The questions asked them to consider how it feels to act against injustice and what stops them from taking action when they can. In turn, the sharing of students' personal stories with injustice can lead their classmates to not only understand how people experience social problems but also imagine what they can do about them.

Students in a different class composed comic strips displaying their own experiences with discrimination (Wei, 2006). They first wrote essays and then transformed them into comics. Some of the immigrant students portrayed experiences they had in their countries of origin—bringing a global awareness to the class. Teachers can ask their students to create print or visual texts so as to share their knowledge and firsthand accounts of social problems.

Or, teachers can prompt students to write about their views of society without requiring them to speak about themselves. One high school teacher, Mama C—discussed in Maisha Fisher's (2005) work—asked her students to read Assata Shakur's autobiography (Shakur, 1987) and then write a "'generational poem' showing links between social and political struggles of people of African descent depicted in Shakur's autobiography and current issues" (p. 116). This assignment both scaffolded opportunities for them to form connections between historical and contemporary examples of injustice and express their own views of society today. Shakur was a political activist and former Black Panther, and students might read her autobiography and then cite their own experiences with racism and segregation.

Student-composed knowledge was shared when students in the race awareness after-school program imagined what ideal schooling would entail. After studying the ways that schools have historically perpetuated inequity between Black and White students, with schools servicing Black students being poorly resourced in comparison to schools serving White students, the multiracial group of students brainstormed what would be in a "perfect" school. Drawing on their own opinions and experiences, they listed positive aspects of the school culture ("letting all kinds of students in the school; get teachers from many backgrounds and cultures"), structural features ("giant gym, elevators and ramps, enough supplies, clean environment"), and details about the curriculum ("sharing our cultures, dedicated teachers"). These ideas were shared aloud in small groups and recorded on large sheets of chart paper. Given that students know what social problems they face, activities where they propose how to rectify these problems enable them to imagine and prepare them to present a clear message during their action step.

Overall, asking students to create and offer their own ideas and stories to their classmates in their pursuit of a civic literacy project positions the students' views as valid and powerful. The culture of schooling often suggests that students are to be passive and that their thoughts are unimportant. If and when student-generated texts are used to help other students explore a particular problem, they can see how youth voices matter.

Students might feel hesitant or self-conscious with respect to their own writing or personal experiences and would, therefore, be resistant to offer their views for public exploration. Or, when they offer their perspectives, their classmates might ridicule them. While it is valuable for students to share their experiences and "define themselves in their own terms," it is necessary that instructional practices be informed by an awareness of potential negative outcomes (Blackburn, 2012, p. 41). Specifically, if students write something that they think is private, it should be kept private, and if students are asked to share their writing or reading publicly, teachers should prepare students for some potentially negative consequences.

This feedback was offered to teachers who invite LGBTQ students to write about their experiences (Blackburn, 2012), yet it can be extended to teachers who ask students to talk about a range of controversial or personal issues. In turn, teachers might allow students to select a part of their self-composed work that they feel comfortable sharing with the class. When using this strategy, teachers prompt students to choose 2–5 sentences that communicate the essence of their piece or whet their classmates' interest in their writing. Students can then choose to read an excerpt that provides them with safety yet offers something that could be significant to the class.

There are ample resources for teachers to integrate into the curriculum during civic literacy projects. Each come with challenges, yet specific instructional moves can be enacted so as to curtail the problems and enhance the possibilities of multimodal learning on social issues. So as to not feel overwhelmed by the options, I encourage teachers to start by choosing two or three types of resources of those presented above. It is also helpful for teachers to propose certain resources that will play primary roles during the problem exploration phase and others to play secondary roles. When teachers form these distinctions, they define the flavor of their problem exploration, and they can plan accordingly. Students will also make suggestions, and their proposals of how the class should learn about the issue at hand will be important to take into account.

PROCESSING THE INFORMATION

In civic literacy projects, students engage with the aforementioned texts in ways that promote their active participation and critique. The multiple forms of text are not there for passive consumption. Instead, students learn to dissect, question, affirm, and critique them as they explore civic problems. Towards this end, this section reviews strategies that can promote comprehension of text and focuses especially on those that promote critical understandings of the texts or help students come into conversation with each other about them. These critical and conversational skills are important in civic literacy projects because the projects present social problems that should be questioned and analyzed in community with others. I bring attention to such literacy skills while also supporting a form of multimodal literacy, outlining how students might encounter problem exploration through reading, writing, composing/designing, and speaking/listening.

Reading

Given my multimodal focus, reading here is perceived of broadly; students read print, visual, and oral texts, and all types of texts require the skills of comprehension and critique. To foster such skills, teachers model thinking aloud when reading a text out loud—a practice called the read-aloud think-aloud. Some key comprehension strategies to model are summarizing, predicting, questioning, and clarifying when they come to a part of the text that they don't understand (Schoenbach, Greenleaf, Cziko, & Hurwitz, 1999). Once these four cognitive skills are explicitly modeled and taught, students can use them while reading in small groups, in pairs, or during independent reading. Small-group, paired, or independent reading allows students to move at differentiated paces when using these strategies.

In order to promote a critical approach, teachers ask students to question the intent of the author when portraying a certain social problem. The skills of critical readers can also be modeled during a read-aloud think-aloud and then prompted using questions such as "Whose viewpoint is expressed? Whose voices are missing, silenced, or discounted?" (McLaughlin & DeVoogd, 2004, p. 58). After these scaffolded steps, students can work to practice reading from a critical stance on their own or in collaboration with others. It is particularly important to foster critical reading skills when reading textbooks. They appear to offer a more unquestionable, official form of knowledge yet, like all texts, are worthy of critique. For example, if students are looking to understand recent unemployment rates, they might turn to history textbooks to study trends of employment from the past. Then, they can question how, if at all, this history of their country's economy is portrayed in the texts.

Eighth-grade students participating in the social justice writing assignment employed such critical reading skills. At the start of the unit, Scott Rosner, their teacher, asked them to read a number of teacher-selected documents on a variety of issues and practice critical reading skills in reference to them. During one lesson, as students read a public letter advocating for the return of soldiers in Iraq, they independently answered the following questions: "Who wrote the letter? What is the letter regarding? Why was it written?" Then, the class reviewed the vocabulary in the letter, shared their answers to the questions in small groups, and discussed them as a whole class. The students' vocabulary work as well as their small- and whole-group discussions promoted their comprehension of the text. The question "Why was it written?" asked students to exercise the critical literacy practice of analyzing an author's perspective, revealing the non-neutrality of text (Powell, Cantrell, & Adams, 2001). To continue this trend of thinking, the students could have also brainstormed opposing viewpoints by questioning "What might the authors' opponents say in response to her letter?" and then read and questioned texts authored by those committed to the pursuit of the war in Iraq. Ideally, reading processes ask students to both comprehend and critique presented materials.

Writing

Writing is a process that aids in students' comprehension and critique of texts during the problem exploration component of civic literacy projects. When students complete quick writes, journal writing, or note-taking (see Daniels, Zemelman, & Steineke, 2007), they create a record of their thinking and develop their ideas by writing them out. Students can write down their thoughts on class readings, highlighting quotes that strike them as important, new vocabulary words, or questions that they have about the texts. When reading narrative texts, students can complete story maps that outline the openings, rising events, key conflicts, falling events, and resolutions of the texts. Graphic organizers such as concept maps, t-charts, and compare/contrast diagrams are helpful in order to show how details in the texts inter-relate.

In order to bring students in conversation with each other about the problem and the texts they are reading, students can share and respond to each other's writing. For example, they might write their ideas on poster-size paper, hung for all students to see. In this method, students each work with their own marker, and they silently write their ideas, responses, and questions about particular texts on the paper. The race awareness after-school program facilitators used this strategy when students recorded their thoughts about pictures from the Jim Crow era on what they called a graffiti wall. One facilitator prompted the students by writing, "Does this happen today?" in reference to a picture of a café that had two separate entrances—one for people who are White and one for people who are Black. Students responded showing varying understandings of how segregation and racism has changed. Comments included these: "It doesn't happen in restaurants anymore but racism happens today" and "It still isn't COMPLETELY over. There are more rich White people than Black. Whites usually get better jobs." Through their writing, students articulated a critique of present-day society and forged a connection between historical times and today. While such critical evaluations of society should be praised, a statement such as "it doesn't happen in restaurants anymore" can serve as the opening for a clarifying discussion of how and where racism appears (Epstein & Lipschultz, 2012).

Students engage with social problems by writing about them. Whether the students write on graffiti boards, class blogs, or their own private journals, writing assignments give students a place to exercise their thoughts in progress. Finally, students can extend the ideas reported in these texts into full-length narrative or expository texts.

Composing/Designing

Students can also explore social problems by creating artistic, visual products that represent their studies of the problems at hand. First, students can document an identified social problem by shooting and/or collecting already published photographs that illustrate the problem in a scrapbook. Then, the students can question what they see, analyzing the problem portrayed. A close analysis of visual texts can begin by prompting students with the following questions: "What do you see? What do you see in the foreground? What do you see in the background? Why do you think the photographer/composer/artist chose to take this picture?" (adapted from Melber & Hunter, 2010, p. 83).

Teachers and students can also work with iMovie video editing software to compile a range of artifacts (e.g., photographs, music, texts) and create a "layered multimodal story" (Schultz, 2009, p. 92) about a civic problem. They could organize the artifacts all throughout the problem exploration process and edit the video as their knowledge grows. More simply, students might compose a PowerPoint presentation displaying their evolving thinking about a social problem. By composing such texts, students articulate and develop understandings of their identified problems. Then, the visual texts can be shown to the whole class, furthering their processes of problem exploration.

Finally, to exercise their imaginations of how their communities might be different, students can build models of structures in their neighborhoods. This approach was used with the students involved in the race awareness after-school program. After the students described what they thought would be in a "perfect" school, the facilitators asked the students to create models of these schools using shoe boxes, cereal boxes, paper, markers, tape, glue, fabric, and other supplies—an experience that asked them to further develop their ideas about ideal schools. Students used visual composition skills to envision better schools, well equipped for learning. As seen in this case, visual literacy experiences might be seen more often in out-of-school programs, as these skills are not prioritized in content-area standards in the way reading, writing, and speaking/listening skills are. Indeed, the race awareness after-school program included a number of pedagogies that might be regarded as distinct from standard school-based learning. However, teachers can learn from these out-of-school programs and consider ways to enact strategies that will welcome students with a diverse set of skills and multimodal preferences into classroom instruction.

Speaking/Listening

Democratic activity is regularly pursued through speaking and listening. Discussion is commonly used in "the marketplace," in the public sphere, so as to bring diverse groups of people together. Participation through dialogue is seen as uncomplicated, as it is used in multiple realms—everywhere from a kindergarten class's discussion of class rules to a staff meeting dedicated to the topic of the new work-site antiharassment policy to a session of the Senate deciding on a new tax code (Parker, 1997). Therefore, the ability to speak and listen is a key skill and is scaffolded through guided oral literacy activities including whole-group and small-group discussion and improvisational dramatic activities.

Particularly important to the forwarding of democracy is the skill of deliberation. When deliberating, citizens acknowledge a shared problem, orally analyze competing approaches to the problem by examining the costs and benefits to each approach, and decide what action to take (Parker, 2003). Effective deliberative forums held in classrooms contain many steps. First, youth learn about a particular problem and varying policy approaches to this problem, enabling them to arrive to the deliberative forum prepared with knowledge on the topic. Then, teachers can open deliberative forums by asking, "How has this issue affected you personally?" (*Teacher's Guide to National Issues Forum [NIF] in the Classroom*, 2001, p. 2.11) Next, the teachers and students review each possible approach by questioning its benefits and drawbacks, and students are asked to propose how they think the problem could be best addressed. The students are responsible both for sharing their own ideas and listening to and building on those of their peers.

For example, picture a class studying the national issue of immigration reform. They are learning about the debate on whether the United States' policies should focus on welcoming immigrants, tighten control of the borders to limit immigration, or adjust immigration laws so that they will promote our economic needs (London, 2013). After reading about each of these proposals, students orally deliberate on the benefits and drawbacks of each one and suggest how the country should move forward. A deliberative dialogue on a more local issue occurred during the park project when the students discussed various ways for park and government officials to fill their park's budget gap and acknowledged strengths and weaknesses of each approach.

Students can also share formal oral presentations about social problems. Here, instead of deliberating as a group, individual students or groups speak to the class uninterrupted about their learning. For example, a student might deliver a book talk to share the main idea of a text he or she read on a chosen social problem. Through this type of assignment, students present their ideas to a community of peers who are prepared to serve as active listeners, responsible for taking notes and responding when the time is right.

CONCLUSION

In this chapter, I aim to support teachers as they envision ways to explore civic problems with students. It is through this exploration that students can build contextual knowledge about their identified problems and articulate civic perspectives beyond those with which they entered the project. If problem identification supports a process of naming, problem exploration supports a process of knowing, and this knowing is essential if civic participation is to be informed.

To review, to build such informed civic perspectives, teachers first integrate a range of multimodal resources that can promote students' civic knowledge. In that democracy requires broad civic participation, as teachers integrate visual, oral, and print texts that can appeal to different students' preferences, they foster democracy. Then, teachers and students read these varied texts and write, speak, and compose new texts in response to them. These activities support students to comprehend, critique, and dialogue about the information the texts offer. Given the plethora of resources and activities to choose from, teachers and students have multiple routes to consider as they pursue the goal of establishing deep civic knowledge.

CHAPTER 4

Action

This chapter offers ideas for how students can act for a better world, raising awareness and provoking change in regard to the problems they have identified and studied. When taking action, youth compose persuasive texts, murals, and videos and work to ensure that these texts reach targeted audiences outside of their classrooms. As action opportunities are scaffolded, youth emerge as powerful agents in the present. Counter to this view, civic education is commonly enacted to prepare students for civic participation in some distant future rather than involve them in civic action at this time in their lives (Biesta, 2007). This chapter presents an alternative vision and illustrates how students can call for change and tackle social problems now.

I have learned how youth can take action by studying the anchor cases threaded throughout this book (see Chapter 1 for their introductions). For example, through the social justice writing assignment, 8th-graders organized and participated in a school assembly where they distributed flyers, gave speeches, and delivered PowerPoint presentations on a range of social issues to an audience of their peers. Cara's presentation focused on McDonald's and the hazards of fast-food eating. While she composed a letter to McDonald's, petitioning them to change their standards, during the assembly, she targeted her classmates, seeking to persuade them to change their eating habits. Of all the presentations, hers was deemed a particular success because of her use of visual images and her persuasive oratory skills. Following her presentation, multiple classmates commented on how she captured the audience's attention: "They were listening! They weren't bored or nothing like that!"; "When they heard that a certain amount of people eat McDonald's they were like, that's too much, and they got into it"; "I think a lot of people got what we were talking about, especially Cara's because it was interesting . . . it was very powerful and it caught people's attention." As seen here, when youth take action, spreading awareness and advocating for change, they can display leadership skills and impact others. In this chapter, I draw from the social justice writing assignment, the other anchor cases, and additional literature, pointing out the potential of various action steps, such as organizing a school assembly, and how they can be extended and modified for multiple classroom contexts.

I open the chapter by presenting four conceptual ideas for teachers to consider when crafting meaningful action steps for students in civic literacy projects. Then, I present six examples of actions and explain how youth have pursued them in various settings. There are endless ways that citizens seek to create change, utilizing the press, the courts, and the streets. Given this, I present a small handful of possibilities for action steps that I see as particularly viable for youth. The chapter concludes with a discussion on how educators and youth can prepare for and reflect on their civic actions.

ENVISIONING MEANINGFUL CIVIC ACTION

Classroom teaching is quite action oriented. Yet, as teachers constantly take action that impacts their students, students are afforded few formal opportunities to impact those around them. When envisioning quality civic action, teachers are challenged to extend the same agency they experience to their students and amplify it so that their students can reach not only those in their classroom but also those outside of it. Below, I discuss how students can send their messages outside of the classroom and present a number of additional, inter-related recommendations for teachers when envisioning meaningful action components of civic literacy projects.

Reaching Outside of the Classroom

In civic action, students send their messages to relevant audiences by speaking, writing, and drawing in ways that can raise awareness and create change. They generate "products for the public," or products that are shared with live audiences (Oyler, 2012, p. 34). In reaching such audiences beyond the walls of the classroom, students experience what it means to work within a large civic sphere and understand how their voices can matter there. They attain a public presence, speaking up about what they have learned through their studies and life experiences. When students articulate and act on their ideas in this way, they can create change for themselves and others.

Students participating in civic literacy projects can think expansively about the range of out-of-the-classroom audiences they might reach. To start, students can seek to reach those with defined authority to correct the problems the students see and create change for many people. They can target government officials, business leaders, and other individuals and groups with decisionmaking power by letter writing, lobbying and/or petitioning. This is what occurred in the park project, as the 7th-graders took action when they wrote persuasive letters to their local assemblyperson asking him to vote for a restored park budget. The implications of engaging power in this way are further explored later in this chapter.

Students can also aim to reach a section of the general public, such as their friends and family, with the goals of involving potential allies and swelling critical consciousness for social change. To this end, students compose and distribute consciousness-raising materials (e.g., films, brochures) that are intended to motivate others to do something in reference to the cause. For example, the students in the race awareness after-school program created a video public service announcement on school inequity that was shown to an audience of their parents and other supporters. The video had the potential to raise the parents' awareness of how school inequity was impacting their children. With specific messaging, such texts can inspire parents' activism on issues related to schooling.

Students might also seek to impact a peer audience within their own schools or communities. In the project focused on sexual health, a cohort of 9th-grade students worked with educators to create a grade-wide safe sex health fair for all 9th-graders. They took action in a way that spread information and awareness about sexual health and how to make healthy decisions to their whole grade. In the social justice writing assignment, 8th-graders communicated their viewpoints on various social problems during an end-of-year assembly presented to their schoolmates from other grades. Through the presentations, they could raise the audience members' awareness and inspire them to act for change in regard to issues ranging from water pollution to poor nutrition in fast-food chains.

In order to meaningfully engage the general public, youth present community members—adults and their peers alike—with opportunities to get involved in the identified cause. In civic engagement, ". . . a fully adequate strategy must address *whomever chooses to listen* and must give those people effective ideas and reasons for action" (Levine, 2013, p. 26, emphasis in original). For example, if addressing the social problem of domestic violence, the *Speak Truth to Power* (2010) curriculum proposes that students "set up a table at a popular neighborhood site and provide information about domestic violence, organizations working to stop it and opportunities for individuals to take action" (p. 42). Through such tabling, students might reach individuals in need of support to leave abusive relationships and motivate others to advocate for antiviolence legislation. Specifically, they might collect signatures on a petition in favor of this legislation to be sent to their elected representatives who will vote on it. Through this kind of effort, students mobilize a base of support (i.e., the people signing the petition) by giving them opportunities to take action and influence a policymaker on their topic of concern.

A similar example of youth building a base of supporters and then targeting a policymaker involved "youth organizers" collaborating during an out-of-school program to improve their schools (Kirshner, 2009). The youth built their understanding of how students experienced school by collecting over 950 report cards from their classmates that recorded their interactions with teachers, security guards, and other school personnel. They then used this data to form their campaign for increased student voice in school, arguing that youth deserved more leadership opportunities and to "'do more than just plan proms'" (p. 418). They took action when they articulated their message in student clubs created to build support for the campaign and at a rally and press conference in front of school district headquarters. Then, they took their grievance to school board members—individuals who could change school policies. The district ultimately agreed that students would help to improve the clarity of school transcripts and set up a peer counseling system, thus achieving a greater participatory role. This example illustrates how civic actions can involve building a base of supporters, in this case through student clubs, and then leveraging that support to target more powerful decisionmakers.

Granted the importance of reaching such audiences, this section is not to suggest that action only transpires when students' voices reach outside of the classroom. Whenever students speak up and present their opinions to their peers, allowing their peers to respond, they are taking action. In its grandest sense, action occurs in the intersection of the individual with the social, or at the moments when individuals take initiatives in social contexts (Biesta, 2007). In turn, it can be argued that students take action when they express their views about a problem during the problem identification or problem exploration phases, potentially informing their peers' views. While students should certainly share their concerns in class, they can also bring their views to a broader public and, in turn, learn that they can make a difference beyond their classrooms. To support this, teachers can encourage students to share their views with their peers and use these activities as stepping-stones to actions that garner more public attention and can ignite a broader process of change making.

Negotiating a Place for Critical Service-learning

Service-learning is a pedagogical strategy that asks students to meet real needs in their communities, directing their attention and actions outside of the classroom, while learning specific academic skills. Examples of effective service-learning projects include a recycling campaign where students organized ways to help their school and community manage trash and an antismoking campaign where students created posters, testified at city hall, and wrote to their councilperson on how he should vote on smoking-related policy (Billig, Jesse, Brodersen, & Grimley, 2008). Through such projects, students have opportunities to learn about social problems and take varying actions to ameliorate the problems. In some ways, this is quite similar to the work one might observe through a civic literacy project, as service-learning projects can involve students in the identification of social problems, research around these problems, and action that reaches outside of their classroom. Indeed, a project oriented around the prevention of sexually transmitted diseases, culminating in a health fair, is identified as a service-learning project (Billig et al., 2008) and is quite similar to the 9th-grade safe sex health project discussed in this book.

Yet, there can be important differences between service-learning projects and civic literacy projects, depending on how much the service-learning asks students to think critically about social problems and take action that advocates for sustainable solutions for many people. As introduced in Chapter 1, civic literacy projects ask students to question and address social problems that affect "us," ideally influencing forms of lasting change through deliberation and other participatory strategies. While this approach focuses on building a collective good for years to come, critics of service-learning explain that service-learning can be oriented too much around simple charity exercises where privileged individuals help individuals with less privilege without fully understanding their experiences (Wade, 1997). These charity efforts can lead students to feel overly self-congratulatory and mainly focus on what they did, not on how others experienced their service or on how they forged a common good.

Following this critique, teachers are challenged to advance an ideal of justice where citizens think past direct service to individuals and consider how problems can be approached at their roots (Wade, 2000, 2001). For example, this means not simply giving a person food for one night, but questioning how food is distributed in the world, why hunger exists, and what we should do to tend to this deep-rooted issue (Ogden, 1999). Such teachers are driven by the following statement:

> It will be important to let the young see that service is not just about altruism or charity; or a matter of those who are well-off helping those who are not. It is serving the public interest, which is the same thing as serving enlightened self-interest. Young people serve themselves as members of the community by serving a public good that is also their own. (Barber, 1992, p. 256)

Here, charity is seen as distinct from taking action for the common good.

However, teachers and students can incorporate charity-oriented service-learning into civic literacy projects and stretch the service-learning to engage students in critical thinking and action for long-term change. Specifically, a charity stage of service-learning can be framed as a first step. This first step not only provides a valid social service, such as the delivery of clothing or food, but also asks students to interact with those who are different from them and ultimately develop a sense of care for others (Cipolle, 2010). At this point, they move away from the charity stage and enter the caring stage. If individuals stay in this caring stage for long enough and thoroughly feel compassion for those they serve, they can become compelled to think bigger about what can be done to ameliorate the issue at hand and act for broader systemic change. Cipolle (2010) explains this trajectory, as can be related to service-learning projects:

> At the charity stage, students are mainly concerned about themselves, how they feel, and what they get out of the experience. In caring, students begin to develop relationships and consider the needs and feeling of others, and they see it as their responsibility to improve opportunities. At the last stage of social justice-activism, students realize that dismantling an unjust society is in everyone's best interest and requires working in solidarity for our common good. (p. 48)

Thus, service-learning that may begin as charity activities can form the foundation for broader social change efforts that include working for the common good.

Working with organizations that assume a social justice-oriented, not charity or even caring, stance helps students move past simplistic models of civic action (Cipolle, 2010). As a result of working with a committee focused on protecting city parks, for example, students would not simply participate in a park cleanup. They would work with the committee leaders to learn about the government agencies that are responsible for park maintenance and question to what extent and why the parks in their neighborhood are different from parks in other neighborhoods. These exploratory activities could lead students to join the committee's campaign that advocates for better oversight and maintenance of all green spaces in their city. When students and teachers partner with such groups, the leaders inspire them beyond charity efforts and towards an examination of the political context of their work and how they might create sustained change. A practical note: Advocacy organizations focused on such long-term forms of change generally enact campaigns that last longer than civic literacy projects, especially if a project is to conclude with the school year or marking period. Given this, teachers and community organizers should work together to determine something concrete that the students can offer during the action phase of their project that fits within the organization's larger action plan.

At the junctures between charity, caring, and then social justice activism (Cipolle, 2010), teachers can reflect on the fact that civic action can be seen on a spectrum. As they support students to move along this spectrum, they challenge students to advocate for a sustainable common good rather than exclusively helping discrete individuals through short-term charity efforts. Thus, a civic literacy project can include service-learning efforts if the service-learning eventually asks students to question how to advance a better life for many.

Engaging Power

While charity efforts largely avoid politics and negotiations with those in power, when students commit to working for long-term political change, they will face the challenge of engaging with power. This involves students asking, "Who has the power to rectify the problem for many and make the change we want to see?" and conducting research to identify key decisionmakers involved in any one public dilemma. Here, students learn how to analyze social and civic structures, determining who controls what, and then direct their messaging to the identified power brokers.

Students can engage many different types of individuals and groups so as to engage with power. In the park project, a class of 7th-graders sent self-composed letters to their assemblyperson asking him to vote for a restored park budget and to challenge the state governor's proposal to reduce park funds. Among the anchor cases in this book, this is the strongest example of youth collectively targeting power. Despite the ways their action step might have been additionally augmented, suggestions that are reviewed later in this chapter, their work signals how students can seek to communicate a shared message with elected governmental officials on local, state, and federal levels. Students might also engage corporations or business leaders if the youth see a problem with the way companies are run. When 8th grader Cara, spotlighted at the start of the chapter, wrote to the McDonald's Corporation, she took action in this way. Finally, if their issue relates to their schooling, students might target school boards (as seen in Kirshner, 2009), superintendents (as seen in Kwon, 2008), or their own school's principal. Overall, in civic literacy projects, teachers and students can look for opportunities to influence relatively powerful individuals who can affect the way the identified problem manifests for large groups of people.

When students communicate with people in power, they can receive a variety of responses. First, the power brokers might ally with the students, potentially having already formed an opinion about the issue prior to their interaction with the students. In this case, the students can influence them to champion the students' cause and promote it widely. Second, the power brokers might react by dialoguing with the students, informing them of the constraints and pressures that they face. In this scenario, students will have the opportunity to learn from those in power and acknowledge that even those with disproportionate power are not omnipotent (Levine, 2013). Third, given that particularly powerful individuals have many groups vying for their attention, they commonly sidestep citizens' requests. If this occurs, students will be involved first-hand in the common phenomenon of citizens' concerns being silently set aside. Finally, the power brokers might actively disagree with the students, who can then gain experience standing in opposition to the views of the powerful. For example, they might encounter their assemblyperson's vocal resistance to engage in advocacy for immigration reform in the context of a project that calls on him to press for more immigrant rights.

Given that teachers are likely to prefer friendly and collaborative relationships with power, and avoid scenarios where their students can be ignored or refuted, I offer in some detail a discussion on the decision to challenge, as opposed to exclusively collaborate with, power.

Challenging those with power is a component of a "youth organizing" model of youth civic participation; in this model, students learn the importance of the less powerful confronting and seeking concessions from those with power (Fehrman & Schutz, 2011, p. 4). This stance reflects the ideas of Saul Alinsky (1971), who advocated the importance of confrontation and conflict in social change. He argued that "Change means movement. Movement means friction" (p. 21) and imagined a free society as an "on-going conflict, interrupted periodically by compromises—which then become the start for the continuation of conflict, compromise, and on ad infinitum" (p. 59). With this view, community organizers value and seek out friction, or conflict, so as to provoke change. They believe that robust participation in civic life, and seeking to change the status quo, almost always entails citizens encountering powerful people and institutions with alterative perspectives and developing strategies that challenge these perspectives.

The idea that social change inherently involves conflict can motivate educators to prepare youth to speak out for change in the face of opposition. Conversely, if teachers exclusively equate civic action with cooperative, nonconfrontational efforts such as charity projects, they run the risk of sidestepping the realities of power in society and evading valuable educational opportunities where students can learn how to embrace the authentic struggles involved in creating change. Indeed, "strategies to build social capital that ignore the reality of conflict do so at great peril"; organizations that focus on community-building and collaboration, and the avoidance of conflict and politics, prevent the development of a base of individuals capable of pressing for broad change when resistance occurs (Warren, 2001, p. 29). With these understandings, teachers can aim to ensure that students have opportunities to learn about confronting power held by various interest groups, individuals, and in politics.

A key downside is that projects that ask students to challenge these forms of power can generate students' frustration and hopelessness, as the students' voices are likely to be dismissed (Kahne & Westheimer, 2006). For example, students who studied the lack of access to health care in their city and tried to get the city to support a new women's health center, similar to those who challenged a state Senate bill that could put students and their parents in jail for truancy, were unsurprisingly met with resistance. The students aimed to change governmental and educational programs from outside of the system, seeking to alter the status quo without the pre-established support of any of the agencies they contacted. In this context they "frequently were turned away, ignored, or in the students' words, 'not taken seriously'" (Kahne & Westheimer, 2006, p. 291).Without people in power to collaborate with, the students reported frustration and hopelessness.

To minimize such discouragement, teachers can use specific strategies to help students manage the realities of confronting power and the related frustrations. First, before executing any action, teachers and students can define success and also define alternate versions of success that are more likely to be achieved. This can prepare students for the possibility that they might not witness their legislator creating the policy they envision but they can feel proud if they achieve a more manageable goal such as mobilizing a certain number of their peers around the cause. Focusing on smaller, incremental wins is a way to build the confidence of youth and keep them engaged (Lewis-Charp et al., 2006).

Second, teachers can ask students to brainstorm ways to collaborate and compromise with powerful public officials, rather than solely expressing oppositional viewpoints. Indeed, organizations can "generate effective power by combining confrontation with collaboration" (Warren, 2001, p. 13). For example, if the students seek to critique the quality of school lunch and find ways to improve it, they can work to identify and integrate the concerns of the school and district leaders into their message. Here, students are not conflict-avoidant, but they do not over-emphasize conflict and acknowledge that those in power have interests to be recognized through negotiation. Civic literacy projects can serve as viable venues for practicing the art of finding a common ground.

Finally, if students experience resistance or silence from their target, teachers can work to ensure that students have opportunities to direct their messages to people who will support them and help them meet at least some of their goals. In other words, if those with power are unresponsive, teachers can still provide opportunities for the students to accomplish tasks that are important to them (Fehrman & Schutz, 2011). This may involve partnering with community-based organizations that are committed to the students' mission and can help them recover from setbacks.

Thus, if a police commissioner most directly in charge of police training does not respond to students' letters and emails that request an increase in the number of hours spent on antiracism workshops, their teachers can direct the students to contact community organizers who are working on police reform and are amenable to working with the students. As the students dialogue with the organizers and take action steps with them, they gain support in the challenging task of confronting power. When students work with "efficacious organizations," form supportive communal bonds with others who believe in their cause, and meet role models who continuously fight for a cause despite the challenges, their hope can be sustained (Kahne & Westheimer, 2006, p. 294). In guiding students to form these partnerships, teachers can develop students' resilience if they are faced with resistance.

Drawing on Student Agency

As with the phases of problem identification and problem exploration, it is essential that students experience agency and empowerment when determining what action steps they will take. Students should consider various possible actions and, when the time is right, determine which possibilities would be most effective or meaningful for them to pursue. They might decide relatively quickly that they want to get others to sign a petition addressed to their legislator and drafted by a local community group that asks for some concrete change in their community. In this case, the students could commit to gathering a certain number of signatures and supporting an already up-and-running campaign. Or it may be more challenging for the students to determine an appropriate target and action step. Students might have to conduct research over a series of days to figure out to whom they should direct their message and how. For example, they might be motivated around the lack of broadband Internet access in their school and realize it necessary to conduct a number of interviews with school personnel to figure out who has decisionmaking power on this issue. Whether their deliberative process is short or long, in civic literacy projects, students assume leadership roles in determining and executing their action.

While it might seem contradictory, teacher guidance is crucial as students evaluate their options and eventually take action. When teachers give authority to students to direct the action component of their projects, they hardly abdicate their own authority; rather, they play important roles in sharing information and feedback to students. Continuing the above example about Internet access, a classroom teacher might know of a city councilmember focused on securing federal funding to expand broadband access in schools. This teacher could lead the students to a news source about this figure and ask them to pursue research about her efforts and consider partnering with her. In these ways, teachers steer students towards assignments that are do-able and confidence-building, thereby ultimately protecting students' civic agency.

Or, teachers can present students with a range of ideas of what might be entailed in their civic actions. Brian Schultz (2008) made this decision with his 5th-graders when they launched an advocacy campaign to get a new school building. Schultz describes his decision:

> Encouraging the students to be active change agents, I introduced them to a book entitled *Civics for democracy: A journey for teachers and students* (Isaac,

1992). I thought the section "Techniques for Participation" would give the students momentum that would allow them to expand their efforts. . . . In small, cooperative groups, the class investigated different ways they could get others involved and influence them to support their cause. (p. 65)

The section "Techniques for Participation" includes ideas such as leafleting, issuing reports, and lobbying. In studying such texts, students can evaluate multiple possible ideas for civic engagement when determining what particular action step they will pursue.

If students conduct research on action steps citizens take to address civic problems in the present and throughout history, they are likely to encounter stories of citizens who have run the risk of arrest and physical harm during civic action. For example, students knowledgeable of the Civil Rights Movement will be aware of the use of sit-ins to protest segregation and how they resulted in jails packed with protestors. Teachers can acknowledge these forms of activism through discussion while ensuring that students do not ultimately choose such action steps during their civic literacy projects. This again illustrates the unmistakable importance of teachers serving as involved mentors who guide students towards appropriate actions. They can explain the danger of risking physical harm or arrest as minors, the problems of pursuing such actions during a school-based project, and the value of many other actions that are likely to be fully sanctioned in schools and out-of-school educational contexts. Just like selecting a text that is at an instructional level for students to read as opposed to one that is inappropriately challenging, teachers hold responsibility to guide students towards meaningful, but not inappropriate civic actions. To direct them to such appropriate actions, teachers can present the possibilities of students writing persuasively, composing politically themed murals, and filming digital videos that present social messages. I present these and other options for viable action steps for youth in more detail below.

After the students have a list of possibilities, they can deliberate over what action steps would be most meaningful for them to take. In this process, they brainstorm the advantages and drawbacks of perhaps three to five possible actions, ranking the options from most to least effective or worthwhile. Whole-class deliberation is particularly helpful if the students will be taking action together. If they are working independently, with each student pursuing his or her own action, or in coalitions, teachers should ask students to brainstorm with a partner or in their coalition about how they should take action.

This deliberation process will ideally ask students to reflect on various complexities of civic action. For example, the deliberation should allow students to evaluate who to position as their target audience (e.g., community-members, peers, elected officials, school leaders) and how to best reach this audience. Furthermore, during such an exploration of their options, if students are confronting those with power, teachers can introduce their students to the terrain between conflict and cooperation, introduced above, and ask students to evaluate action steps where they might express their concerns, as well as enter negotiations with those in power. Students can experience the same decisionmaking process as community-based advocacy groups who determine how and when to utilize different tactics.

Depending on the scope and the goals of the civic literacy project, students might choose anywhere from one to many action steps. In Brian Schultz's class, where the students were advocating for a new school building over an entire school year, they took action when they created and circulated a petition, wrote letters to political figures, and launched a website on their cause (Schultz, 2008). Through these and other actions, Schultz and the students gained much media attention and built a base of supporters (including Ralph Nader). In comparison, in the park project, where students advocated for increased funding for a local park, they enacted a singular action step: They wrote letters to their local assemblyperson. They were able to pursue this action step in a few weeks. Whether selecting one or many actions, depending on what seems most tenable for any one moment, student agency is ignited when students have influence over what and how they communicate to the public.

TAKING ACTION

This next section of the chapter presents six examples of civic actions that students can pursue during civic literacy projects. They are a handful of the myriad options for civic action, as this section serves to begin, not conclude, a conversation about what is possible when youth reach out of the classroom so as to influence lasting forms of change.

As for literacy development, the selected options illustrate how civic actions, reaching a range of potential targets, engage students' print, oral, and visual literacy skills. Students should reflect on which modality is most likely to reach their target audience and then communicate their messages accordingly, through writing (print literacies), speaking (oral literacies), or composition (visual and digital literacies). For example, digital videos posted on Facebook are likely to capture the attention of youth who commonly use social media sites to build community and knowledge. The action step should also reflect the students' literacy skills and interests, as they may be best positioned to create texts in a particular genre. They might have recently studied how to write effective personal narratives and now wish to create an anthology of personal narratives on their experiences related to discrimination so as to raise others' awareness about the issue. Teachers can view the action step as a means to build on and expand students' literacy skills while also aiming to reach the identified target audience.

Persuasive and Investigative Writing

Students are commonly required to write persuasive and/or research-based, investigative texts in their English language arts classes. Therefore, such assignments can be seen as natural entry points for students to engage in civic action. Instead of students' conducting research and writing persuasive texts that never leave their personal writing portfolios, students can write nonfiction texts so as to convince public audiences to pay attention to particular injustices and do something about them.

Students' persuasive writing can take many forms. Students might compose letters to be sent to legislators; op-ed statements for school, town, or regional newspapers; leaflets which students can distribute in public areas or on car windshields; or blog posts on a student-created website or the website of an organization focused on the students' identified issue. In all of these forms, their work should be argumentative so that it communicates a particular message and encourages the target audience to adopt a particular view and act in a particular way. Their texts might persuade their superintendent to allow students to carry cellphones in schools, a local university to conduct information sessions in their high school explaining their application process, or a legislator to vote for a change in voting laws.

During the park project, 7th-graders wrote persuasive letters to their local assembly member to ensure that the park budget would permit all of the services generally offered—including maintenance of indoor and outdoor pools, classes, sports teams—to indeed be offered. Following their teachers' instruction, the students' letters addressed the following topics: facts about the park, reasons for the cuts, consequences of the cuts, and suggestions for how to address the deficit. While each letter was unique and included information and suggestions each student selected as most important, students generally concluded their writing with a call for help. For example, students wrote as follows: "Please consider the people. We need your help to stop this budget cut. . . . You can understand how we must feel"; "Vote against the budget"; and "I believe with your support we will be able to help the community get our beloved park back." They used direct language to appeal to their assemblyperson and compel him to challenge the proposed budget.

Days after their letters were placed in the mail, a note was posted on the community website dedicated to this fight for a full park budget from the assemblyperson himself, announcing to his constituents that the park budget had been restored. Upon hearing this announcement, the students yelled and applauded—they were thrilled. The following week, two students, representing the class, announced the victory at a school assembly held for the 7th grade at which students were displaying different end-of-year projects. After explaining how they learned about the budget cuts, considered different action steps, and chose to write letters, they proudly presented the results of their civic work:

> The outcome of this situation was actually very good. The assemblyman wrote a letter saying the park's funding will be restored. We are proud that our class proved people wrong; kids can make a difference in this world! I'm also proud that we wrote intelligent and convincing letters to support our park, which is very important for us who live here.

The persuasive writing assignment garnered the students pride in their civic work. The students' reactions may be critiqued in that they focused on the impact of their letters, yet they had not received any recognition that their letters were read. While this valid point is explored further below, I see benefits in the way the students seemed to learn that citizens can collectively express a grievance through persuasive writing.

Students' persuasive writing is enhanced when they conduct research, seeking evidence to defend their arguments. Thus, if students are writing to their city's taxi commission with the claim that taxi drivers ignore Black and Latino/a residents in their community and demonstrate a bias towards picking up White residents, they should find and include testimonies from community members or reports that establish this. Students use research, likely pursued during the problem exploration phase, to illustrate the problem and propose what can be done to make a change.

Students' research might also be presented in a piece of journalism, in which case they operate with less interest in persuading their audience to adopt one clearly stated view and more interest in raising awareness about their identified problem. A variety of such investigative pieces is presented on Youthwire (see www.youthwire.org), an alternative media source that posts pieces created by Californian youth from underserved communities and aims to reach local audiences as well as policymakers throughout the state. One youth author wrote a piece that aired her community's concern about the possible overcrowding of health clinics with the advent of the Affordable Care Act in January 2014 (Europa, 2013). She cites the views of health care professionals and community members. This piece seems intended to inform public opinion about the act and, if subsequently directed towards them, could incite legislators and health care workers to address or comment on the possible overcrowding. More generally, the article illustrates how youth can use their voices to raise awareness and encourage critical thinking after conducting research on pressing social issues.

Poetry and Narrative Writing

While persuasive and investigative writing generally follows a predictable form, students can also write in creative genres so as to communicate social messages. In this section, I illustrate how students write poetry and personal narratives to this end. Drawing on a range of model texts, students compose and then publish or perform creative texts, reaching large and small audiences.

Through one high school program, Poetry for the People (P4P), college "student-teacher-poets" (STPs) work with English teachers during the school day and guide students as they write poems about their personal experiences that can make an impact (Jocson, 2006, p. 130). Illustrating the benefit of partnering with outside organizations, here classroom teachers, STPs, and students work together for approximately 4–6 weeks analyzing, creating, and disseminating poetry. The dissemination occurs through the creation of a published class anthology and a public reading.

At a P4P public reading at a community cultural center, one student wrote and performed a poem documenting his experience being racially profiled by the police (Jocson, 2006). In reading his work to an audience of parents, teachers, students, and other supporters, he embraced an opportunity to "literally—speak out and be heard," as explained by the researcher who studied this program (p. 144). Poetry is a genre through which students can question social norms, write about provocative topics, and capture an audience's attention through the performance of the final pieces.

At times, students will compose poems to be presented with other poets to communicate messages about a topic of shared concern. For example, a public conference entitled Immigration and Education Conference: Envisioning Schools, Communities, and Policies of Acceptance concluded with a poetry performance, Voices of the Journey: A Spoken Word Celebration of Immigration Experiences. Of the 10 presenters at the performance, two were high school students and four were university students. They wrote and submitted poems in response to the following call: "Tell your story, have your voice heard, speak up, speak loud, speak your story!" In turn, the poems performed spoke of the authors' experiences as immigrants or knowledge of immigration experiences.

The spoken word celebration fit into the conference's broader vision for participants to learn about the complexity of immigration and how it impacts education and to ultimately be inspired to advocate for greater justice for immigrants. Held in 2011, it was well-attended by students and community members as well as individuals who influence policy at the New York City Department of Education, the city's Office of Immigrant Affairs, and the City College of New York—the location of the conference. Therefore, when students compose texts for such conferences, and specifically public poetry readings, they have the opportunity to reach broad audiences. Teachers should keep on the lookout for such events organized by community-based organizations and hosted in local bookstores and universities.

Students can also write personal narratives about their experiences with social problems to raise awareness and create change. In an urban high school, low-income students of color took on the problems of drugs and murder to address as a class through their civic engagement project (Rubin & Hayes, 2010). After considering various ways to counter these problems (i.e., holding an event in the school, putting up signs in the neighborhood, attending Board of Education meetings), they compiled and published an anthology of texts on their daily experiences with the problems. Entitled *Listen: An Anthology of Student Voices*, the "emotionally powerful document" contained stories and photographs (Rubin & Hayes, 2010, p. 370). The students exited the project feeling that they had participated in meaningful action. One "loved" the project, and another valued the way their teacher let them "express our feelings." This shows the power of scaffolding opportunities for students to publicly share their own narratives. While traditional media sources routinely misrepresent youth as problematically contributing to social problems rather than reflecting on or addressing them, youth can represent themselves by self-publishing their narratives on websites or alternative media sources (Kelly, 2006). Through the narratives, they can share their own experiences with the high school dropout phenomenon, teen pregnancy, drug use, and so forth. Their perspectives can be eye-opening for their audience members and shape their views about these problems and how they can be addressed.

When students are writing poetry and narrative texts, a key element of the action occurs when students ensure their work reaches outside of the classroom and initiates a chain of events that encourages change. If students orally present their work, as in the cases of the poetry performances above, students should invite certain groups and individuals whom they want to have present for their readings. School leaders—principals and superintendents—as well as other community figures can learn from the students' stories. Similarly, if they disseminate their work as print pieces, as seen in the case of the anthology on drugs and murder (Rubin & Hayes, 2010), or as digital pieces on websites, they can create a list of groups and individuals who will get personal copies of or links to the texts. These processes ask students to be deliberate about who they want to experience their work. Finally, given the creative nature of poetry and narrative writing, the audience may be moved by the pieces but not clear on how they should get involved. In these cases, students can open or close their pieces with clear calls to action in which they advise their audience how to advocate for change in regard to the problem addressed in their work.

Speeches and Presentations

While poetry performances serve as an important type of creative oral presentation, this section focuses more explicitly on speeches and presentations
that are expository and persuasively direct the audience to a particular finding. They are delivered at community forums, assemblies, press conferences,
and other public events and forward clearly stated claims. The presentations
can serve as a means to raise the audience's awareness or influence its future
decisions. For example, if students studied the smoking trends in their high
school, student speakers representing the class might present their call for a
new school-based antismoking campaign at a school board meeting. If their
problem exploration phase ended with students assuming different stances
on the identified issue, they could organize a panel where students present
the value of different approaches to the controversial issue (e.g., gun control
policy). Through this action step, they collectively share a range of oral
arguments, allowing those in the audience to clarify their own views on the
issue and determine which next step to take.

The social justice writing assignment concluded with an assembly in
which eight students delivered oral presentations on their topics of interest so as to influence their peers. Scott told the students that their writing
projects should be taken "out of the classroom" so that they could "affect
things" and "make a change." And Scott explained that "most of them decided that they can impact other students." In turn, he invited the 8th-grad-
ers to present their work during a school assembly. Here, I will spotlight two
students' oral presentations—Margaret's on trash collection and Darion's
on the high school drop out phenomenon—to illustrate what students might
include in such work.

Margaret delivered an oral presentation, accompanied with PowerPoint
slides, on the mismanagement of trash collection in her city. On her own
time and with her own cab fare, she took pictures of neighborhoods in her
city to compare the trash. She found that the streets in wealthy neighborhoods had no garbage in the street while in her own neighborhood, which
had a lower socioeconomic status, garbage was left to create clutter and a
poor odor. Margaret's PowerPoint presentation displayed her photos and
concluded with specific action steps. A slide entitled "Ways we can help
clean up our neighborhood" called on her classmates to "make a plan to
have a big clean up project . . . protest outside the office of community
affairs . . . write open-letters to the sanitation department." These suggestions show that she recognizes the problem of trash collection as needing
remedy through service activities, such as neighborhood cleanups, as well
as through advocacy for systemic change as a result of protests and letter
drives. She also drafted her own letter to the local department of sanitation.

Darion, an English language learner, also shined during the assembly as she called on her peers to stay in school, countering a high school dropout phenomenon among Black and Latino/a youth. The speech included a cautionary anecdote about an impoverished high school dropout and a call for action: "We are the next generation and we have to improve"; "Americans think that Puerto Ricans, Dominicans, Ecuadorians, Mexicans are good for nothing, and we know that is not true." Sadly envisioning Latino/as as not-American, Darion still forwarded a vision for how Latino/a youth could forge a good future for themselves. A Latina teen herself, she identified the target of her project as "Hispanic or Latin teens" and called on them to acknowledge stereotypes that frame them as underachievers and then move past those stereotypes and stay in school. Adding to her action step of delivering a speech, for more sustained change, Darion could have organized her peers to reach policymakers in the Department of Education to recommend what could be done to support students across the city to stay in school. At this moment, she focused on reaching her adolescent peers by speaking at the school assembly.

Oral presentations can include dramatic components where student activists perform scenes presenting the need for change. In one high school, junior and senior high school students performed a dramatic scene when they interrupted a welcome-to-school assembly for 8th-graders to yell discriminatory slurs such as "chink" and "faggot" to each other (Darts, 2006). Then, a second set of students rose and yelled "stop!" Next, the students left their roles and this staged charade; explained their antibias mission; and initiated "focus groups" for the incoming students about discrimination, bullying, and violence. This performance was organized as a part of the school's larger effort to stand up against hate in the school. The dramatic presentation at the start of the assembly likely served as a motivating, thought-provoking influence for the 8th-graders—the target audience—who would then arrive to the focus groups ready to talk. When delivering a formal speech or a dramatic performance, students can consider a range of strategies they might use to capture their audience's attention when presenting oral texts.

Workshops and Lobbying

Not only are youth capable of delivering speeches or presentations to audience members who are positioned as listeners and observers, youth can also design interactive activities that ask participants to talk and formally commit to forms of social change. Whether in workshops with community members or lobbying meetings with government officials, students can communicate with others asking them to explore their views on social problems and adopt certain behaviors or concerns. In these scenarios, students use their listening and speaking skills to engage others in consciousness-raising conversation.

Students in a Gay-Straight Alliance led antibias workshops with incoming 9th-graders in a high school committed to making the school a safe, supportive place for all students, regardless of sexual orientation (Mayo, 2013). They participated in the *Think Before You Speak Campaign*—"a nationally recognized program designed to help students avoid derogatory phrases like 'that's so gay' and make word choices that more clearly express what they truly mean to say (ThinkB4YouSpeak, www.thinkb4youspeak. com)" (Mayo, 2013, p. 271). The workshop leaders led sessions during freshman homeroom periods. This example shows the potential power in positioning youth as educators and how such youth can draw on the work of larger campaigns like *Think Before You Speak* to guide their action steps.

Students in this same school also participate in a Lobby Day at the State Capitol where they meet with local government officials and ask them to support gay rights. One issue they have addressed is the right for all people to marry, straight and gay. Prior to such a lobbying meeting, students can mobilize their peers to sign petitions or write persuasive letters and then request a meeting with the policymaker to deliver these documents and discuss their concerns in person. During the face-to-face meetings, students can ask politicians to answer their questions, express their current stances and concerns, and commit to certain actions.

If students are working to get an audience to agree with a particular viewpoint during a lobbying meeting, as in this case of lobbying for gay rights, it is important that students are united in their perspective. If students have adopted a diverse range of perspectives on an issue, it will not move any of their viewpoints forward if they share such a range of perspectives with a governmental representative. Lobbying is successfully pursued when citizens with a common cause articulate it together. Therefore, teachers and students should determine whether they are united enough in one particular message when deciding whether their action step should include a face-to-face meeting with someone who could make policy-oriented decisions about their chosen issue. If the answer is "no," it might be more worthwhile for students to write persuasive letters where they can articulate their own viewpoints (see Peck, 2013) or hold a phone party where students call their representatives on school phones or their cellphones to share their own personally crafted messages.

When students organize community-based workshops that are usually less formal than lobbying meetings, youth can engage participants in drama exercises so as to help them explore and gain critical consciousness about social problems. Exercises related to Theatre of the Oppressed are helpful to this end, as this type of liberatory theater is committed to the exploration of and solutions for social problems (Boal, 1979). Through one exercise, participants pose in ways that illustrate a problem or form of oppression and then alter the pose and use their facial expressions and body positions to show their ideal and the absence of oppression. One drama troupe composed of high school students have used Theatre of the Oppressed techniques with students from Maine to New York to explore issues of bullying, teacher scolding, and racism; their work prompted critical conversations among the student participants as well as themselves (Duffy, 2006). In one workshop, they asked middle school students to create images of what it felt like to be a student in their school. This exercise asked the students to think about the antagonism and hostility that exists between students and teachers and imagine how the student body could experience more peace.

During workshops and meetings, youth utilize exercises, questions, and presentations that they believe will engage the audience in dialogue. Whether talking with their peers or adults, these types of action steps provide opportunities for them to motivate others to consider the weight of a social problem and what can be done about it.

Murals

Visual literacy skills can play essential roles in civic action. Students might design T-shirts with compelling messages or banners to be used at school or community-based events. This section talks about the possibility of students' creating murals for public display, as murals can be mounted for long periods of time, serving as consciousness-raising tools for those who view them.

A 9th-grade class guided by the nonprofit organization Urban Youth created a mural in reference to their chosen social problems—teen pregnancy and gang violence. Zaire, a youth worker from the organization, scaffolded the students' experience creating the mural. First, he suggested that the class design a mural to be hung within the high school so as to influence the students' peers. He was an artist and had the skill to support students through this process. Then, with the students' buy-in, he asked the students to determine what would be on the mural. For example, in planning a street scene outside of their high school, they considered what a pregnant teenager portrayed on the mural should be doing and what emotion should be represented on the part of her mother.

The students also spent two periods discussing the print message that would be written under their mural. At the start of the first period, the students seemed to be more focused on the issue of gang violence, offering two options: "Gangs don't give you power, your mind does" and "If there is no peace, there is no unity. If there is no unity, there is no progress. If there is no progress, there is no future." In response, Zaire suggested that they have multiple messages around the canvas. The class voted and decided to stay with one message and continued to negotiate what it would be. Aiming to focus the students, Zaire suggested that "the mural is about future choices." The students then started experimenting with the words "choice" and "decision" and concluded with the tagline "You have a great future ahead so make the right choices." This tagline had the potential to send a clear message to the students' classmates, involving them in their campaign regarding gang life and teen pregnancy. At its conclusion, the mural was displayed at a reception organized to celebrate the students' work, and plans were made to hang the mural in the school.

Other students seek to mount their murals outside of the school, thereby targeting a larger and more diverse audience. This was seen in a case of high school students who wrote to a city government official to secure a site for their public mural about local community problems (Fehrman & Schutz, 2011). When they received no response from the official, their "coach"—a volunteer guiding the project—connected the students to a nonprofit urban arts organization that displayed the mural outside the organization. Here, they learned about the role of city officials and the frustrations often involved in working with people who hold such power yet figured out a way to have their voices heard. Indeed, their mural ultimately communicated a powerful message described here: "The mural, titled 'Liberty for All but Not for Us?' challenged citizens and the powerful to 'visually listen' to students' grievances about social inequality and police oppression in their neighborhoods" (Fehrman & Schutz, 2011, p. 8). In their action step, they learned to navigate political obstacles and project a statement of social critique into their community.

Finally, murals can be used as tools to express cultural pride and empowerment. An example is a mural at Roosevelt High in Los Angeles, California:

> [The mural] included images of indigenous people to acknowledge the communities' indigenous history and build pride, as well as depictions of young people marching in protest for youth rights, the Dream Act, and educational justice. . . . Placing empowering murals on the walls of a school invites the community to learn from the knowledge produced by youth and artists and advocates for members of the Chicano/Latino community. (Morrell, Duenas, Garcia, & Lopez, 2013, p. 139)

The mural acknowledged both concrete social issues and the community's power to advocate for justice. Such murals can influence those in power, or key decisionmakers for the city, if students and teachers create public events and invite such individuals to view them. However, at their essence, they serve the role of building the political and social consciousness and empowerment of the students and community members who view them daily.

Filmmaking

Finally, youth can create videos articulating social messages, using their visual literacy skills to call for change. While a variety of technologies could support youth filmmaking, the ease with which youth use digital cameras and upload digitally recorded films to the Internet make digital filmmaking a particularly appealing choice for youth and educators. Furthermore, these digital texts can reach large groups of people as they are posted on different websites.

One 11-year-old created "Yuck: A 4th Grader's Short Documentary About School Lunch" (Maxwell, 2012), portraying the poor quality of school lunches and the difference between what the education department advertises and what is actually served. The film was shown in multiple film festivals. In addition, *The New York Times* reported on this student's efforts to use digital filmmaking for social change (Sen, 2013). Not only did the *Times* coverage spread Maxwell's message to the public, it also included a comment on school lunch from a spokeswoman for the education department, illustrating how the creation of films can ultimately hold authorities accountable.

While Zachary Maxwell worked with his father after school to create the film, filmmaking can also be supported in educational settings including English language arts and social studies classroom instruction. In these cases, teachers assign students the tasks of gathering footage or dramatizing events that portray social problems and ensuring that the films communicate clear messages. For example, in 9th- and 10th-grade classes in Los Angeles, students composed digital video public service announcements (PSAs) critiquing Arizona's SB 1070 bill (Morrell et al., 2013). The bill allowed enforcement to request the citizenship papers of anyone suspected of being an undocumented immigrant and impacted the elimination of ethnic studies. The students first studied this bill using primary and secondary sources and then took action by creating films in opposition to it. In one film, students enacted a classroom scene where they questioned their teacher as to why a more diverse set of ethnic groups was not represented in their textbook. After the absence was attributed to SB 1070, conversation continued, and then the film concluded with a call to action.

The project on SB 1070 motivated the students and involved them as active, empowered participants. The students directed much of the PSA as they wrote the script and recorded the film multiple times to ensure it sent their desired message. Students who had not been previously engaged in schoolwork stayed late after school to work on this assignment. The video was ultimately shown at the National Council of Teachers of English (NCTE) convention, where it could potentially influence teachers to integrate the voices of the members of multiple ethnic groups in their curriculum and critique legislation that limits such portrayals.

In the race awareness after-school program, focused on urban racial segregation, students also created a film-based PSA calling for greater equality in school funding and efforts to bring White students and students of color together during the school day. The audience of their film was mainly comprised of parents, who were proud to see the 4th- and 5th-graders' critical consciousness and could embrace the youth's call to ensure their social exposure to students of different races. It could have later been passed on to policymakers who influence policies on school integration and funding.

Student-created videos can be readily shared with multiple audiences. As well as making presentations at conferences, youth have shared videos at public forums at City Hall, at meetings or receptions for the public, on Facebook pages, and on the sites of schools and organizations committed to airing youth voices (Morrell et al., 2013). Youth use the Internet as a primary site for communication and knowledge development (Moje, Overby, Tysvaer, & Morris, 2008), and therefore students may be particularly drawn to the ways that they can utilize the Internet to distribute their videos and articulate their own messages of social change to varying constituencies. As individuals and groups receive the films, they can consider the youth-composed messages embedded in them.

All of this work supports a call regarding the centrality of media texts, such as films, in social change efforts:

> [We] need to consider media literacies as central to the project of civic engagement. That is, if our students are to become full participants in civil society, they will have to be able to understand the media they inherit, but they will also need to be able to produce various genres of media to communicate with others locally and globally. (Morrell et al., 2013, p. 170)

While youth consume endless amounts of media messages, they must also have opportunities to create their own media texts. The digital world is a venue primed for the dissemination of such texts, and youth can take advantage of this as a means to communicate their concerns. Furthermore, as teachers ensure that students engage in "the use of participatory online tools and digital resources," during civic education projects, their work emerges as "student-centered," as this is where youth interests lie (Jansen, 2011, p. 38). Educators can draw on this thinking to encourage themselves and their students to integrate digital films into their action steps.

PREPARING FOR THE ACTION

Civic action is effectively executed when teachers devote days, if not weeks, of instruction to prepare students for it. Just as with the problem identification and problem exploration phases of civic literacy projects, in preparation for civic action, teachers play key roles mentoring and supporting students to make change. To start, I encourage teachers to ensure that students have (1) models of other meaningful civic actions to analyze and (2) workshops designed to develop the skills needed for their action step.

Models

As students plan for and enact an action step for their civic literacy project, they advantageously study models of other youth and adult activists taking similar action steps. They might analyze the process these activists pursued when preparing and executing their action if a description of this process is captured in film or narrative. Or they could analyze the product, or action step, itself. For example, if the students know they want to produce a digital video on a concern they have about their school, they could read *The New York Times* article about Zachary Maxwell (Sen, 2013) that summarily reviews how he created the film critiquing school lunch and/or view the film itself. The article presents the steps he took: He filmed 6 months of school lunches and edited the footage with his father's assistance, he selected and integrated the use of costumes and special effects, he calculated statistics of how infrequently the healthy items on the school menu were served, and he determined where to show the statistics within the film. Then, in watching the film, the students would be able to witness the product that came from this work and name the qualities that made it effective.

Additional resources present other models of civic action steps. As presented above, Youthwire presents scores of articles written by youth that contain messages for social change. These articles can serve as models of journalism, persuasive writing, and narrative writing. The winning videos of the Speak Truth to Power Student Video Contest are posted on www.speaktruthvideo.com. Here students can view films such as *Modern Slavery and Sex Trafficking* (2013), created by students in the Young Women's Leadership School of Brooklyn to raise awareness about these social problems, which was awarded the grand prize of the contest. Finally, teachers can share stories about the adolescents portrayed in this book taking action in a range of different ways. When students are exposed to such models, they gain opportunities to analyze the work of others who have reached audiences with clear social messages so as to determine how they will do the same.

Skill Building

Alongside analyzing models, students often need to develop certain skills to ready themselves for their civic action. For example, before delivering a speech to a public audience, students benefit from workshops where they practice making eye contact, speaking audibly, and pausing for impact. Such skills and practices are fostered by teachers who acknowledge that effective action does not magically occur—skill development for effective action is necessary.

During a skill-building workshop, teachers model a particular skill and then enact exercises where students practice it while receiving feedback—praise and corrections—from their teacher and peers. Or guest teachers can attend the class to teach a particular skill in which they have expert knowledge. For example, imagine a poet who routinely performs at poetry slams teaching a lesson on using tone to convey a sense of urgency through the reading. The poet could model this skill and then ask students to practice reading their poems in this way to a classmate. As the students read, the poet could circulate among the students and comment on their tone while reading.

Teachers can predict a list of workshops that will be necessary once students determine what action step they want to take. Each workshop might focus on a discrete skill, or present a set of related skills, that the students will need in order to effectively execute the action. Then, as the students are working, it will be clear what additional workshops are needed. For example, if the students are composing persuasive statements on the use of fracking in their town to be posted on a public blog, and their teacher sees that they are not using persuasive language adequately, a workshop on this skill is necessary. Ongoing assessment helps teachers stay attuned to students' areas of strength and need and enact instruction that supports them accordingly.

REFLECTING ON THE ACTION

As students bring their civic action into the real world, it should be evaluated to determine to what extent change is occurring and what challenges remain. If scaffolded carefully, students' evaluations of their work can lead them to feel committed to addressing lasting injustices through civic work during their immediate project and in the future, whether they deem their immediate action step as successful or not. With such a perspective, even when it appears that the students are creating change, proving that civic structures are benevolent and yielding, students are able to critique remaining social problems and identify new roads of action. Or, if students feel that they are making little change during this project, they are able to brainstorm how they may address their identified problem, or other problems, differently.

One immediate step teachers and students can take to adopt this view of their civic work involves assessing their impact after any one action step and crafting next steps—processes fostered as students address the following questions. Reflection on these questions can be done through small-group exchanges, whole-class discussion, or journal writing as students pursue their action steps. Below, I explore the importance of each question and illustrate its potential impact in reference to some of the strengths and areas for growth of the park project's action step of writing persuasive letters to a local assemblyperson.

Who Did We Influence?

First, students can recognize the people they may have influenced as well as those they sidestepped when they ask, "Who did and didn't we influence?" In this process, students track the responses and silences that they receive after they take any one action step. Some governmental offices send letters acknowledging receipt of communications. If students post civic messages on websites, they can monitor who responds to them and in what ways, or students might organize a sign-in sheet for people who attend workshops or events that they hold. Whatever the mechanism, students learn about who is paying attention to their work, or not, through such tracking devices.

After the 7th-graders in the park project sent persuasive letters to their assemblyperson, asking him to vote for a restored park budget, they learned that the budget would be restored. While the project concluded with a wave of satisfaction, the students never received a response from the legislator in regard to their class's letters and therefore were unable to fully track the success of their action. A strength of their action was that they identified a clear target and therefore could tailor their letters to appeal to his perspective. To build on this, the students might have further reflected on how they could have ensured more direct influence on or contact with the assemblyperson. Specifically, the students might have requested a face-to-face meeting with the assemblyperson or tried to contact him over the phone, as these types of meetings provide venues for community members to press for specific answers to their questions. If these encounters occurred after the budget was restored, the students could have questioned him on how he would continue to protect their park or other local services.

In comparison, in a high school class portrayed in Oyler's (2012) work, students wrote letters protesting the expansion of a power plant and were informed by a community-based organization that their letters made a difference, leading a city agency to also oppose the plant. The teacher reported, "So we're all feeling pretty good right now" (Oyler, 2012, p. 61). Through their contact with the organization, the students had reason to believe that they were heard. Ideally, students adopt a sense of how they touch people through their action and use this information to envision their next action step.

What Made Us Strong?

Second, reflection on questions including "What made us strong, and what limited our strength?" can help students recognize factors that influence their impact. One such factor is the extent to which students work in collaboration with other citizens. Civic power emerges through alliances, and social change comes when groups of people work together to challenge injustice.

In the weeks prior to the park project students' sending their letters, a community-wide campaign was unfolding that involved a petition, a website, and the partnership of local legislators. The students' mission to restore the park budget was made strong by the fact that multiple groups and individuals were publicly working on behalf of this cause. Yet classroom time was not spent reflecting on these alliances, and most students interpreted the impact of their letters in isolation of the broader community-wide effort. If such reflection had occurred, acknowledging the breadth of the campaign and strength of the alliances, the students would have better understood why the park budget was indeed restored and why, without such alliances, they may have been less successful. Also, this reflection would likely have prompted the students to take more collaborative action with the larger community-wide campaign.

When reflecting on the factors that influence the success of any one action, students might raise a number of additional issues, aside from the presence of alliances. For example, they may point to the timeliness of their work or the medium they used to express their message as elements that influenced their strength. In general, students' awareness of strengths and liabilities will help them ensure that they seek out certain conditions, such as the establishment of alliances, when pursuing civic action.

What Is Ahead?

Finally, students can plan next steps by asking, "What is now ahead? What opportunities and threats are pending?" This kind of reflection helps students consider how to move forward after any one action, identifying lasting problems and needed action steps. Specifically, they can conclude their projects listing new or existing problems to address and audiences and alliances to engage.

As for the park project, with budget allocations, when one agency's budget is spared, it is likely that another agency's budget is even further limited—a condition often requiring advocacy. In turn, if a civic literacy project involves budgets, students might choose another line in the budget to defend, or, they might pledge to continue to be watchdogs for their original area of focus, ensuring fair delivery of any social service (e.g., the maintenance of public parks). Positively, when interviewed at the conclusion of the park project, students spoke of their desire to continue to civically engage within their community. To build on this, the 7th-graders might have had more opportunity to collectively consider specific next steps in class.

As students propose their subsequent action steps, even if they will not be carried out within that school year, their efforts illustrate that democracy must be continuously pursued. They can embrace a long-term commitment to civic action as they acknowledge that achievements or setbacks are not final; new obstacles and opportunities are always ahead. In this way, civic involvement is framed as a marathon, not one short-term project, or sprint.

CONCLUSION

Civic action stems from citizens' commitments to provoking change. In turn, it is in this phase of civic literacy projects that youth reach outside of their classrooms and project a message to a broader audience, involving others around their visions of change. Their audiences can then learn about the power of informed youth voices, all while the youth are similarly learning about their own capacities to civically engage. Furthermore, through the action phase, students gain the opportunity to reflect on the impact of their actions and how to carry their commitments to social change forward. These steps are essential as citizens work to foster democracy and social justice now and in the future.

CHAPTER 5

Tensions in Civic Education

Now that I have introduced the three essential phases of civic literacy projects—problem identification, problem exploration, and action—I use this chapter as an opportunity to explore three tensions that may arise for teachers as they progress through these phases. I focus on tensions regarding (1) the balance between individualized and collaborative work, (2) the balance of self-advocating for one's community's needs and adopting the concerns of others through solidarity efforts, and (3) how teachers integrate and address civic issues that generate various forms of civic controversy. I draw on multiple cases of youth civic engagement to show differing ways educators and students can address these tensions.

TENSION 1: INDIVIDUALIZED VOICES AND COLLABORATIVE PARTICIPATION

Every student has had a different set of life experiences informing his or her civic interests. As a result, students will naturally be motivated to work on a wide range of social problems. Teachers can be motivated to address students' diverse interests and scaffold opportunities for them to share and build on their individualized forms of knowledge. Teachers can also craft opportunities for students to work together and collectively pursue research and action in ways that play down their individual stories. Students might form coalitions, small working groups united by common concerns (e.g., police brutality), and engage in community outreach together (Bomer & Bomer, 2001). Or students can work as a whole class or even as a whole school on a project. Given the potential for students to draw on their individualized experiences as well as the value of collective participation, educators are left to question how to foster these processes during civic literacy projects.

Individualized Voices

The social justice writing assignment provided robust opportunities for the participating 8th-graders to independently voice and follow their own civic pursuits. This independence began when Scott Rosner, the teacher, asked each student to choose his or her own topic for the assignment. Then, each student selected genres (e.g., speeches, letters, posters, and brochures) for their work that they predicted would reach their identified target audiences. Given the way this differentiated the students' work, during many class periods for the remainder of the project, students worked on unique tasks. For example, on May 11, Margaret edited her letter to the department of sanitation on the problems with trash collection, Cassie considered how to integrate self-authored poetry into her project on abortion rights, Scott conferenced with Eliza on crafting a powerful opening for her essay on domestic abuse, and Frank researched where he could send his editorial on standardized testing. While some students received feedback from their peers and Scott, they largely pursued their own agendas.

During the opening weeks of the unit, Scott thought that the students would form coalitions around common goals—in line with the model in *For a Better World: Reading and Writing for Social Action* (Bomer & Bomer, 2001). However, he revised this vision when he saw how many problems the students wanted to address. He explained, "You can't really plan what will happen because it is based on what the kids come up with." In turn, he put aside his idea for coalition building when he felt it didn't reflect the fact that the students were identifying so many different ideas. At the close of the project, Scott reflected that he was glad that the students had worked independently, commenting that collaborative participation would have "slowed things down instead of pushing things forward." He also felt that he had provided ample opportunity for the students to work in groups throughout the year and learn collaborative skills, and this project did not need to replicate that same participation structure.

Students valued the independence that they were given during the unit. At its conclusion, one student, Eva, shared advice for teachers desiring to enact such civic-oriented writing projects in the classroom: "Let the students pick what they want . . . if they get to pick it, it will be something they have pride for so maybe they will do well." Similarly, Michael explained, "One thing I would tell teachers is, don't disagree on any topic your student chooses to do. You might disagree with it [at first], but go along with it, you might change." Here, the students expressed that they valued identifying their own problems to work on. In one instance, a student might have formed a coalition with her classmate, or been encouraged to do so by Scott, yet she chose to work independently. Specifically, she chose domestic abuse as her topic when she found out that another student was focusing on HIV/AIDS. She said about her classmate, "When she said the same topic, I said, no, let me change it to domestic violence . . . because she might get the same information and then it will be the same thing, so I wanted to change it." The social justice writing assignment allowed for this type of independent decisionmaking.

In the end, students presented texts on varied topics and in varied genres for an audience of their peers at a school assembly. Some presented oral texts such as speeches and PowerPoint presentations. Others distributed hard copies of brochures or hung posters that communicated messages of social change. The students' individualized interests were clear.

Collaborative Participation

As an alternative to the independence offered in the social justice writing assignment, students might work collaboratively to identify and address one issue, as was seen in the safe sex health project. At the start of this project, facilitators from a nonprofit organization, Urban Youth, asked the students what they wanted to change in their community. Through this dialogue, they named their common concern that they had too many unanswered questions about sex. In turn, they developed a safe sex health fair to bring needed information to themselves and their classmates. This unified action step symbolizes the shared nature of their project.

Reflecting the program's interest in collaboration, the most commonly used participation structure throughout the project was small-group or whole-class work. First, every Urban Youth session opened with a "check in" during which each student responded to a question (e.g., "What is your favorite cartoon character?"). This process allowed all voices to be heard at the start of every class. Also, leading up to the culminating event—the safe sex health fair—the students were organized in groups to work on particular tasks. For example, they worked in small groups to create graphs charting adolescent sexual behavior to post during the health fair.

The facilitators worked to create tasks that would interest the students, as they recognized that not all students would be motivated by the shared topic alone. For example, when creating the graphs, students were assigned roles emphasizing their drawing, reading, or writing skills. One facilitator explained this as follows:

> I think very often the kids will like the topic of the project, and that is why they want to be involved. And, there are kids where the topic is not entirely relevant to them, but they have something to contribute.

If all students are going to be working to address a singular issue, it is important that teachers offer students varying opportunities to contribute to the collective mission.

Explaining the impact of all their collaborative work, Mona, a student, stated, "We got to work together . . . we had so much to do in so little time so we all had to work together and rush through it and push all the negative things to the side and just focus as one." Similarly, Tanisha, the lead Urban

Youth facilitator, praised the students for their ability to work together. In response to my inquiry at the end of the school year about what she thought the students learned, she replied, "I think they learned to work together as a team to accomplish one goal." This type of learning is afforded when students collaborate and address a singular civic problem.

In a separate high school program, with a similar collaborative approach, students participated in public forums in which they expressed their individual experiences with teachers, security guards, and other school personnel, ultimately arguing that they wanted more leadership opportunities in the school (Kirshner, 2009). They employed a perspective of "collective agency" in which they advocated for their self-interests by working together towards a common goal (p. 414). The safe sex health project granted the students similar opportunities for "collective agency."

Suggestions for Teachers

Teachers have reason to value and balance opportunities for individual *and* collective work in their classrooms. Viewing the issue on a theoretical level, Dewey (1897) calls on educators to maintain a dual interest in children's independent "powers" as well as their "social relationships":

> In order to know what a power really is we must know what its end, use, or function is, and this we cannot know save as we conceive of the individual as active in social relationships. But, on the other hand, the only possible adjustment which we can give to the child under existing conditions is that which arises through putting him in complete possession of all his powers. (pp. 5–6)

Children must be aware of their individual abilities, but they can only understand them when they are of use in a community. Here, children are seen as individuals in social contexts who acknowledge the people around them that inform and witness their actions.

Given the value of this balance in educational contexts in general, civic literacy projects yield unique educational opportunities for students to learn the value of joining or building collective efforts so as to make social change. As individuals build social relationships and organize together, they gain power, and therefore, civic literacy projects can teach students the importance of forging alliances with people and groups. Particularly in the context of the subordination of low-income African American, Latino/a, immigrant, indigenous, and poor White communities, the members of these groups often experience few individual rights, and so they work together to express shared political demands (Collins, 2010). Indeed, grassroots political organizing gives marginalized groups a form of resistance against social, economic, and environmental injustice. Therefore, if students independently identify problems, teachers can construct opportunities for them to work with and present their ideas to others during the problem exploration and action phases, thereby joining a larger community.

When the students in the social justice writing assignment presented their work at a school assembly, they engaged in a setting where they could build a base of collective support. Specifically, Cara's presentation on McDonald's illustrated what happens when students think about ways to involve others in their cause. First, she directed her messaging to the audience members and called on them to avoid fast food. Second, she created a plan to evoke their attention. Prior to the assembly she said, "I think they will be excited 'cause I'm not going to read word for word. And the pictures will make them get that visual eye on it so they will interact a lot." Cara ultimately utilized various mediums to stimulate the audience's attention. Her final presentation included oral text, visual images, statistics on fast-food consumption and obesity, and her message to "make the right decisions to be healthy"—and it was deemed very successful, as presented at the start of Chapter 4. One of her classmates explained, "It was interesting . . . it was very powerful and it caught people's attention." Despite the fact that Cara pursued a project on her own self-identified problem, her public action step showed her ability to communicate with and motivate others around her cause.

Cara's action step as well as most of her classmates, might have included an even broader collaborative approach. Namely, following her presentation, she might have leveraged her classmates' interests in the problematic fast-food industry by asking them to all sign a letter she wrote to McDonald's, or sign a letter penned by an advocacy organization, asking the company to change the ways it produces food. Indeed, she would have had more opportunity to ignite social change if she had joined or organized a larger campaign. Students can work with students from other classes or schools or a community-based organization in order to experience the value of collective power.

As students work and communicate with others during civic literacy projects, engaging in social and collaborative efforts, they can also be supported to draw on their independent interests. Teachers can construct opportunities for them to see how their own voices are embedded within the collective concern. For example, while all the 9th-graders worked together to form one safe sex health fair, individual students advocated for and helped to organize particular aspects of the fair that they felt were more or less important, based on their own individualized experiences.

One student felt very strongly that sexual violence should not be discussed and didn't come to the weekly sessions for weeks to protest this possibility. She was ultimately persuaded to join the class when a teacher discussed the importance of her knowledge. He explained his interaction with her as follows:

I said, "Well, you need to come. You need to really come and guide them towards a different direction." And she eventually did . . . and that's when we had to have these conversations about how when we are presenting these things we have to be very sensitive to how we bring things up because you may not know if a person sitting next to you has had a negative experience.

He encouraged her to recognize the importance of her own story and take responsibility and initiative in shaping the direction of the fair. The fair ultimately focused on avoiding teen pregnancies and the contraction of sexually transmitted diseases, not sexual violence. This illustrates that even when the class has a communal focus, students should have opportunities to share their individual viewpoints and know that they are heard. As another example, if all members of the class are writing letters to communicate one shared message to a local representative, each student can insert his or her personal story about why this message is important. These efforts allow the students to make use of their independent experiences within collective efforts.

TENSION 2: SELF-ADVOCACY AND SOLIDARITY

A second question teachers and students face during civic literacy projects is whether to work on a problem that most directly impacts other people or most directly impacts themselves and how to pursue either option. This points to the difference of working with a solidarity model, where students form ties of solidarity to those who are different from them, or a self- or community-advocacy model, where students advocate for their own immediate needs (Epstein & Oyler, 2008). If working in a self-advocacy model, students address oppressive situations that intimately characterize their lives. In these projects, students have clear opportunities to form strong connections to their own communities and see themselves as change makers within them. Through a solidarity model, students work with those whose social, political, and economic realities are often quite distinct from their own but whom they connect with based on the notion of "justice for all." This perspective is often required if students want to address a problem that is directly manifesting in other parts of the world, not their own. Both options are valuable, as is a combination of the models, as illustrated below.

Self-Advocacy

Sometimes problems that immediately impact the students' lives are prioritized in civic literacy projects. In these cases, students are given the opportunity to work on civic problems that are concrete and obvious to them, and, in doing so, they advocate for their own immediate needs and those of their local community members. This is what occurred when the 9th-graders created a safe sex health fair. To review, students shared their belief that too many students at the school, including themselves, had pressing questions about sex yet not enough forums to find answers. In creating a health fair, with the guidance of facilitators from an organization called Urban Youth, they sought to meet a perceived need of their community.

Interestingly, another safe sex health fair had recently occurred in the school, organized by the school social worker. That fair was critiqued for not being youth oriented. A student, Paula, explained: "We had a fair before but it was 'whack' . . . they were just talking about the diseases. They didn't make it fun. So, we did another one so we could interest the students more." To that end, they had a disc jockey playing music while students walked around tables staffed by organizers from nonprofits where they could get brochures on safe sex, key chains, candy, and other gifts. The teachers concurred this fair was "very different . . . very much more youth based." There was an absence of youth-centered dialogue about sex, and the students were proud to fill that void for themselves and their peers. As a next step, the students might have considered how to contact policymakers in their city's department of education to ensure the lasting presence of relevant, student-centered sex education in their own and neighboring schools.

The self- and community-advocacy model illustrated in the safe sex health project reflected the Urban Youth program's mission. The program director, who oversaw multiple projects running throughout her city, explained their goal:

> When something in their life happens that they want to change, they have the tools and they have the skills to change it. Whether or not it is 'I don't like the high school I am going to,' or 'My parents are divorced and I don't want to live with my dad anymore and I really want to live with my mom,' or 'I want to change my major in college,' whatever it is, they understand that they have the power to make that change. If it is something on the level of 'Oh, there is that torn down house and I really want to see if I can turn it into a garden,' then they will know that they have to make the phone calls, figure out what their resources are, rally their peers, and do all those things.

The leaders were committed to scaffolding opportunities for the students to advocate for changes in their lives.

In keeping with this mission, the students identified a problem in their school and worked for changes that would help them and their classmates. Through the use of an advocacy model, students engage in "pro-social and positive civic activities to improve their own communities" (Ginwright &

Cammarota, 2007, p. 698). This type of community-based work is illustrated in the safe sex health project.

Solidarity

At other times, students will want to address a problem that is not immediately impacting them but that is significantly impacting others. This is likely to happen if students address a social problem that is manifesting in a faraway country. For example, students living in the United States who responded to the 2010 earthquake in Haiti had the opportunity to adopt the plight of the Haitians as their own. This type of work, where students learn about injustices that manifest most clearly countries away, is evident in a unit on global human rights (Gaudelli & Fernekes, 2004). Through the unit, high school students developed empathy for the victims of human rights abuses, such as those impacted by the state-sponsored violence during the military coup in Chile in 1973. As students pursue such studies, they learn about and address the social and political realities of different peoples and potentially gain opportunities to question their own forms of privilege.

Students can also work in solidarity with people who are their local neighbors yet whose lives are quite different than theirs. For example, in many urban areas, housing for wealthy residents is in close proximity to housing for low-income residents. Students of privilege might work in solidarity with low-income neighbors to advocate for affordable housing. A similar type of solidarity work was structured through the race awareness after-school program, organized by a nonprofit group called Beyond Today. In this project, White students attending privileged schools had opportunities to express solidarity with students of color whose school conditions were less than equal.

Specifically, during the after-school program, students came together for programming from three urban schools. The greatest disparity was between Elementary Central, servicing predominantly White students from upper-class communities, and Lark Elementary, servicing predominantly students of color from communities of lower socioeconomic status. There was a large gym and cafeteria in Elementary Central, and it was routine for students to use computers in their classrooms. Teachers were often provided with teaching assistants. Comparatively, the students from Lark Elementary had few opportunities to use resources such as computers, and they reported that their bathrooms rarely contained toilet paper—a sign of the shameful condition of the school. The after-school program organized opportunities for the students to compare the conditions of their schools, both by visiting them and through subsequent written and oral reflections. These learning activities provided a context for all students to recognize the differences in their schooling experiences and to build ties of solidarity.

During student interviews, Alice, a White student from Elementary Central, named her privileged schooling situation. She said, "I didn't know that school education could be so unfair. When I went to Lark Elementary, to their building, it was so, so different from ours . . . we have different materials than they do." While her statement would have been sharper had she identified more qualities of the school differences, it illustrates how students might name the diversity of life experiences around them and begin to break traditional silences about privilege (Epstein & Lipschultz, 2012).

All of the students, those who were suffering from substandard school conditions as well as those in a privileged school environment, advocated for school change when they created a PSA for their culminating action step. The PSA called for greater equity between schools and proclaimed the value of "mixing it up," or building friendships and relationships across lines of race and class. The process of creating the video seemed to provide the students with a fertile opportunity to deepen their connections and solidarity with each other, which had been growing throughout the year. One facilitator observed, "Everyone's ideas were combined and helped to successfully create a PSA," and another noted, "All of them worked so well together. They were so determined and bold." This project spotlights the possibility of students' working in solidarity for a more just common good.

Suggestions for Teachers

Both the self-advocacy and the solidarity models of citizenship education have value. Self-advocacy projects position students as watchdogs for their own communities and advocates for their own needs. In his survey of literature on engagement between schools and urban communities, Schutz (2006) argues for such youth involvement in local struggles so that youth can form close connections and commitments to their neighborhoods. In comparison, through solidarity models, youth seek out, listen to, and affirm the experiences of those who are different from themselves (Nieto, 1994). Building such affirmation and solidarity asks students to apply sophisticated dispositions in their interactions with other citizens.

Both models might also raise concerns. During the problem identification phase, teachers might be hesitant about focusing exclusively on immediate issues requiring self-advocacy because they wish to structure opportunities for students to learn from those who are different from themselves. This is particularly the case when working with privileged students, as teachers might intentionally ask them to form empathy with and address the needs of the less privileged. Conversely, teachers may be wary of asking students to form solidarity with others and focusing exclusively on issues that do not directly impact the students, out of the fear that they are too abstract for students to grasp. Also, if students do not fully understand the experiences of those most directly impacted, they can problematically presume to know what is best for other people (Wade, 1997).

One way of addressing these concerns and drawing on the benefits of both models is for teachers to look for opportunities to combine elements of the self-advocacy and solidarity models. If students identify a problem that impacts them directly, they can also be connected to those who want to work in solidarity with them. For example, the Urban Youth facilitators who guided the safe sex health project connected the high school students with a corporate organization that provided volunteers for the fair. This created an opening whereby the volunteers could form ties of solidarity with the youth. Yet, their relationship lasted 1 day—the day of the fair—and therefore the structures were not put in place for strong ties of solidarity to emerge. However, ties of solidarity can begin to form when students connect with others who adopt the students' cause as their own, possibly from other schools or outside organizations.

Alternatively, if students identify and choose to work on a problem that is more distant from their day-to-day lives, in order to forge ties of solidarity, teachers can design opportunities for the students to meet and dialogue with those who are advocating for their own needs. If they are addressing an issue that is global in nature, such as the AIDS epidemic in Africa, they can connect with African organizations doing AIDS advocacy work. They can then design an action step that is aligned with the concerns and desires of the African organization. Similar partnerships can be forged on a local level. This was possible in the race awareness program when the students all worked to raise awareness about school inequity. The students who directly experienced the less-than-equal school were positioned to advocate for their own rights, and the students in more privileged schooling situations were working in solidarity with their peers.

Teachers can also illustrate to students the connections between social problems in their immediate communities and those that students perceive as more distant by building knowledge about the systemic injustices that inform local, national, and global problems. Scott's approach in the social justice writing assignment introduced the possibility for this. During one interview, he explained, "A global vision can be found as a result of a local instance." For example, students might be concerned about the asthma rates and pollution in their neighborhood, and their interests could lead them to research and connect with countries worldwide in the same situations.

Fostering the possibility for these connections, Scott introduced the students to civic concerns that exist locally, nationally, and globally both during the problem identification and the problem exploration phases. To address local realities, students collected ethnographic observations of their urban neighborhood in their notebooks. Scott also introduced injustices and responsive activism beyond solely that in their community. For example, the day after a series of rallies around the country calling for a revised national immigration policy, Scott prompted the students' thoughts on the rallies. One student commented that in comparison to California, their city did not have multiple rallies. Scott responded as follows:

> That is a good point. There was a lot going on around the country but not much in this city. It is interesting that there was all this organizing, and here, a place where there are so many immigrants, there wasn't anything. Instead of me telling you more about this, I want you to do the research.

With this directive, the students began to read the delivered newspapers that covered the rallies throughout the country. Such instruction provides students with information they would not have otherwise, broadening their civic lenses, and positions them as capable of addressing problems that have ramifications for their lives as well as the lives of others.

TENSION 3: CONTROVERSY AT A DISTANCE
AND CONTROVERSY AT HOME

Finally, teachers and students are keenly aware of how civic problems elicit controversy. All civic issues can be controversial. Yet no issue is inherently controversial; they are socially constructed as more or less controversial in different communities at different times (Hess, 2009a). Given this, teachers and students might intentionally seek out, or be most drawn to, civic issues that stir little initial debate among the students, placing controversy at a distance. If this is the case, it is nevertheless important for the students to know how to analyze a range of viewpoints others hold about their identified problems. Alternatively, teachers and students may choose to address a political issue in a civic literacy project on which there is a broad divergence of opinion in the class, welcoming it as a controversy. In this section, I aim to support teachers as they evaluate how and when to introduce students to debated perspectives regarding their identified civic problem.

Controversy at a Distance

The park project was driven by students' common dedication to restoring the budget of their neighborhood park so that all of its services could be offered. Questions of whether the park should be spared from the state budget cuts garnered little controversy, and the students embraced a shared cause to "save the park." This dedication likely stemmed from the 7th-graders' affiliations to the park, which they saw as under attack. They explained that the park is like their "home" and that it is "not only a park . . . it is part of us." In their interviews, numerous students told stories about birthday parties and family events that they celebrated in the park. Indeed, through their advocacy, they could impact their own summers, the next of which was due to begin in weeks; depending on whether the budget was restored, the students would have a pool to enjoy and sports teams to join or not.

Yet, as the students' concerns were building, a debate was simultaneously unfolding about how the state should go about funding all of its programs. As in many times of budgetary deficits, legislators and other involved citizens were torn about whether they should increase taxes so as to meet the budget, advocate for more efficiency in government so as to trim spending, cut services, or use other methods to meet their expenses. Given this debate, the teachers, Deanne Holly and Lucy Oaks, both acknowledged the students' viewpoints, encouraging them to use their voices in defense of the park, and also carved out some opportunities for the students to name and explore the controversial question of how the state should best cover its budget.

The teachers' commitment to exploring this question is most illustrated in their enactment of a deliberative forum on possible ways to ensure full funding to the park. They asked students how the budget gap should be filled. The students proposed three solutions: (1) raise service fees, (2) open a souvenir center to create revenue, and (3) hold a benefit concert or basketball game in the park. Then, they brainstormed the benefits and challenges associated with each approach. While the students' three proposed solutions were not representative of those authentically debated by the legislators, the exercise introduced students to the contested question of how the budget should be met.

Following the activity, the teachers were highly enthusiastic about how the students grappled with this question. Deanne described that after airing the different viewpoints, along with the benefits and limitations of each one, "it got heated. . . . They said things like 'No, you can't do that' and 'No, I like that idea better.'" At another point in the interview, she affirmed this point: "They were passionate. And, they were allowed to disagree—that is so strong! The kids were allowed to say, 'I don't agree with you. Here's my point of view.' And, they listened to each other." It came time to go to lunch, and Lucy said, "They wanted to keep on going! I was like 'You guys want to continue? Don't you know its lunchtime?' 'No, no, no, let's finish. We gotta finish this.' They were so really into it." The students were eager to air their views on this class-created controversy of how to best fund the park.

On other days, students expressed additional options about how to address the state budget shortfall, further illustrating their awareness of different, and potentially competing, stances. Randy said, "They should take away more from a big park, than just a little park," framing their local park as a "little park" that should remain fully funded. Julio suggested that they raise taxes on the rich or on gasoline. Finally, the students read texts acknowledging the rationale for why the park programs needed to be cut, including a letter from the state governor, and how this decision would help address a large shortfall in the overall budget. Through exposure to these ideas, students considered different ways that needed dollars could infuse the budget. Some also expressed newfound awareness of the strains that legislators face, and as one said, how they "suffer" when trying to meet many different citizens' needs.

While the park project united the students around a common concern for the park and the importance of a restored park budget, initially placing controversy at a distance, by the end of the project the students were aware that this was not a simple issue. They shared multiple viewpoints on ways to meet the budget in class discussion, and many of them presented their suggestions in their letters to their assemblyperson. This learning was scaffolded when the teachers structured opportunities for the students to acknowledge that there are debated responses to budget decisions.

Controversy at Home

At other times, the students in a particular class or group will hold divergent viewpoints on a civic issue, and as they air their different perspectives, the issue is framed as controversial right from the start. Deanne and Lucy experienced this the year before the park project. At this time, students participated in a civic project on the potential expansion of a nearby university and the related gentrification of their predominantly low-income community. This was a controversial issue within their city and within the class. Indeed, as the students surveyed local community residents on their feelings on the university expansion during the problem exploration phase, the community members' testimonies made plain the controversy. Some residents felt strongly that the university would bring more jobs and social capital to the community while other residents felt that the expansion would surely displace them and would show little respect for their history and culture. The students also articulated this diversity of perspectives, and, for the remainder of the project, the teachers and students discussed the university expansion as a controversial issue, cognizant of the varied opinions it evoked.

The following school year, a similar diversity of views emerged about the university expansion. In the weeks before the park project began, the teachers distributed a survey prompting the students to share their thinking about the expansion, as they thought they might continue to focus on it. Students' responses to questions, including, "What is your opinion about the university's growth? What would you like to tell others about the university's growth? What would you like to tell the people who run the university?"* surfaced their opinions. Students in opposition to the expansion wrote comments including "Do it somewhere else" and "I don't like it" while students in favor called it "amazing" and a "great idea." A number of students expressed balanced points of views, referencing both strengths and weaknesses of the expansion plan. For example, one wrote, "I think it is good and not good. It's good because there are more schools. It is bad because people are going to lose jobs." Given this, the teachers considered exploring multiple views on the expansion and then allowing students to write and speak their own perspectives. They thought that the students' persuasive writing could be sent to local politicians, leaders at the university, and students' parents.

The teachers' confidence to teach this controversial issue grew after they learned of websites that articulated different viewpoints on the expansion. The university's website posted text clearly in support of the expansion and all its benefits. To counter this, an advocacy group objecting to the expansion posted descriptions of the social, economic, and environmental hazards the expansion would bring. Finally, a development corporation outlined a stance that would allow for the expansion but with compromises. Upon learning of this information, Deanne proclaimed, "This is great because now we can get this off the ground. . . . We already have the stances that we could use to present to the kids and . . . have them branch off to see where their opinions lie." Lucy proposed that they make a "chart to juxtapose the viewpoints . . . to show that people have varying different points of view." They composed pedagogical ideas that they felt would fruitfully frame the issue as controversial throughout the problem exploration phase.

Soon after, they decided to focus on a different problem—the budget cuts that would impact a local park—as they felt that this timely problem "really excited" the students. The ensuing project, discussed above, ignited less initial controversy within the class. Yet, the teachers were prepared to focus on a question that generated clear controversy within the community and among the students.

Suggestions for Teachers

During civic literacy projects, students can address issues on which there is broad disagreement inside their classroom or take up concerns that do not garner such immediate controversy. If, following conversations with colleagues and students, teachers frame an issue as controversial right from the start, teachers can validate students' and community members' diverse viewpoints by assigning readings from different perspectives, bringing in guest speakers, and prompting students to air opposing viewpoints all throughout

---

*The original questions included the name of the actual university, which I replaced with "the university" to protect the participants' anonymity.

the problem exploration phase. This is what the teachers planned for when thinking about how they would teach the university expansion. Then, when taking action on an issue that continues to elicit controversy among the students, students can work in coalitions, organized around common viewpoints, to articulate particular stances to targeted audiences. Or, as a result of robust deliberation, students might establish a common ground and determine one shared perspective to articulate on the identified issue, even when there is initially great controversy within the class. To this end, teachers would need to dedicate ample instructional time to foster the development of this common ground.

Conversely, a teacher might decide to place controversy at a distance and instead build on students' common concerns. This is what occurred in the park project. The students set out to collectively protest the budget cuts and advocate for increased funding to the park. In these types of projects, students engage in the problem exploration phase seeking to understand the nature of a shared problem. In the action step, students will likely be able to articulate a shared message.

However, even in cases when students are united around an issue that they do not see as controversial, in civic engagement, controversy is rarely far away. Teachers can intentionally structure opportunities for students to encounter it. While the students in the park project were motivated to collectively speak out against the park budget cuts and engaged in weeks of research and writing to help them with this task, they dedicated time to exploring the debated and controversial question of how to increase the available funds for the park and balance the state budget.

Embedded in this tension of how to engage controversy is the argument that issues should not be inappropriately framed as controversial just for the sake of teaching controversy. For example, while some may wish to teach the question of whether global warming is caused by human behavior or a natural event as a controversy (Laviano, 2007), global warming should arguably be framed as a problem caused by human behavior, as this is what science has come to show and because the stakes are so high (Hess, 2007). Teachers can support students to develop a common perspective of global warming as a fact and a product of human behavior, instead of engaging them in the now-dubious debate about whether or not it should be a source of concern. Then, after affirming this common cause, teachers can explore the authentic controversy over how public policymakers should address global warming.

If controversy is altogether avoided, important learning opportunities are also avoided. Discussions of controversial issues in schools are praised for the way they teach deliberative skills and for the way they help students better recognize and appreciate the diversity of opinions citizens hold on political issues (Hess, 2009a). Therefore, without such learning opportunities, students are allowed to ignore other people's experiences and perspectives.

To illustrate—imagine a class working on a street-improvement campaign for their civic project. After collecting data on the street on which their school is located and interviewing community members, the students determine that the street would be enhanced by adding recycling bins, mailboxes, and a basketball court. They create maps that illustrate their desired changes and present them to their local assemblyperson. The assemblyperson is impressed by their unity and their ability to advocate for a common cause.

Throughout the project, however, the teachers are aware of an issue that may have provoked disagreement among the students; at the corner of the street is a public housing complex. Some students live in the complex, and other students believe that it is a scary place to be avoided. At the conclusion of the project, the teachers are pleased that the students never raised a conversation about public housing in class because they are not sure of how they would have handled this potential controversy. Yet, in avoiding this conversation, the students holding negative assumptions about the projects and about low-income community members had no opportunity to explore their assumptions.

After uniting the students around their common desire for basketball courts, the teachers might have fostered a dialogue about public housing and the controversies this issue raises. For example, some think that there is too much crime in the projects and a worthwhile goal is to advocate for mixed-income housing, doing away with public housing. Others advocate for some needed improvements of the housing projects without disbanding them, noting that families and communities have built histories in public housing complexes and their rootedness should be respected. In pursuing this conversation, the students might have expanded their views about public housing and learned from others—products of discussions on controversial issues.

CONCLUSION

This chapter is about recognizing tensions that exist in civic engagement and establishing informed approaches to these tensions. Every civic literacy project can illustrate its own reconciled approach, balancing (1) students' independence and the value of collectivity, (2) the role of self-advocacy and solidarity efforts, and (3) the differing types of controversy civic issues raise. Ideally, as teachers work to strike balances, they do so with an awareness of the implications of their decisions, an awareness that this chapter is intended to promote.

CHAPTER 6

Designing Units to Promote Civic Literacy

This concluding chapter illustrates how the three central phases of civic literacy projects—problem identification, problem exploration, and action—can be fostered in one classroom-based unit organized around clear long-term objectives. Civic literacy projects should not be conceived as tack-ons to the curriculum, executed without consideration of strategies of sound curriculum design. They should be thoughtfully planned and enacted by teachers making use of research, theory, and practical insight. This chapter serves towards this end, as I demonstrate how to apply such pedagogical knowledge to civic literacy projects.

Specifically, I walk teachers through a multistep process that they can use to design a unit that involves a civic literacy project. First, I discuss how the process can open when teachers determine their curriculum orientations, or the values that will guide their unit design (Eisner, 1985). Then I detail how teachers establish standards-based long-term visions for the unit, craft key performance tasks that ask students to be active in their learning, and plot a learning plan—including day-to-day lessons. I discuss throughout how in crafting a unit plan, teachers can both think about ways to support the students to move towards the long-term objectives and remain watchful to identify what is proving to be meaningful for the students so that they can integrate their needs and interests into the unit.

Novice teachers are likely to find this chapter's focus on unit design helpful as they begin learning curriculum planning skills. Indeed, I wrote the chapter with an audience of beginning educators in mind. Experienced teachers should read this chapter as a review of principles of unit design and an illustration of how such principles are applied to civic literacy projects.

REFLECT ON A CURRICULUM ORIENTATION

Teachers design and enact curriculum with various motivations, each suggesting a different orientation to the larger purposes for schooling (Eisner,

1985). As debated since the start of the twentieth century, teachers and educational leaders have favored (1) curriculum that imparts time-honored knowledge to youth through the study of a uniform body of information, (2) curriculum that supports students' individual needs and interests, (3) curriculum oriented around a series of particularized skills that prepares students to engage productively in the workforce, and (4) curriculum that asks students to critique and improve society (Kliebard, 1995).

Teachers draw on the fourth approach to adopt a "social reconstructionist" orientation to the curriculum (Eisner, 1985; Kliebard, 1995) and enact civic literacy projects. This orientation suggests that curriculum should position students as change makers in regard to the social ills that they see around them. It asks them to name and analyze social problems and then develop the skills and knowledge needed to do something about what they see.

While the term *social reconstructionist* was originally used in the early, formative years of the field of curriculum and teaching, a helpful articulation of the social reconstructionist curriculum orientation set in modern times can be found in Henderson and Gornik's (2007) work on transformative curriculum leadership. Henderson and Gornik persuade teachers to operate under a "curriculum wisdom orientation" to create curriculum that not only develops students' understandings of the subject matter but also asks students to practice the values of a democratic society. Towards this end, teachers develop projects that ask students to embrace "the freedom necessary for the making and remaking of a public space for dialogue and possibility" (Henderson & Gornik, 2007, p. 49). The skills of questioning, dialoguing, and recognizing differing points of view are central as students ideally develop their democratic selves and social understandings. Given its focus on subject matter, self, *and* society, teachers can use the curriculum wisdom orientation as a platform from which to consider how classrooms can be places for students to think about the world in democratic and justice-oriented ways.

Drawing on a curriculum wisdom approach, as an articulation of a social reconstructionist orientation, does not foreclose opportunities for teachers to reference other curricular orientations. They might couple a curriculum wisdom approach with one that puts less attention on the role of schooling in the protection of democracy and instead focuses on the more individualistic interests of the children or the pressing demands of standardized tests (Henderson & Gornik, 2007). If teachers assume that curriculum can provide a place for youth to change the world, it will arguably be easy, or at least feasible, to find a place in the curriculum to teach standardized test skills. Conversely, if a teacher begins with an exclusive focus on academic content knowledge and standardized tests—orientations that value discrete sets of knowledge and often singular correct answers—it can be difficult to create curriculum that asks students to look at the broader society and determine their own stances on civic issues. Beginning with a curriculum wisdom approach makes an acknowledgment of other orientations possible.

For example, teachers might be committed to a curriculum orientation that prioritizes exposure to what they see as time-honored knowledge and the reading of canonical texts in their English classrooms. They also wish to enact a civic literacy project that involves students in social change. In this case, they can use a canonical text as a jumping-off point to address a social issue in students' lives. For example, *To Kill a Mockingbird* (Lee, 1960) is a text on racial discrimination, and *The Crucible* (Miller, 2003) centers on the issue of religious and political freedom; therefore, as students read these texts, or after they do so, they can pursue civic projects on the present iterations of the same civic topics (Beach et al., 2012).

Another possibility is for teachers to effectively pair classic texts with up-to-date nonfiction texts, prompting students to examine social issues portrayed in both. In one case, 12th-grade students read *Fast Food Nation: The Dark Side of the All-American Meal* (Schlosser, 2001) and compared it to what they learned in the classic, muckraking text *The Jungle* (Sinclair, 1906/2001)—engaging in a curriculum that raised important questions about the food industry (Beach et al., 2012). The teacher used this unit as a starting point for a service-learning project through which she intended for them to "uncover what it means to stand for change and begin their own projects that center on social justice" (p. 101). Therefore, the unit asked the students to study civic issues, a process hailed in the social reconstructionist curriculum orientation, as well as the craft and content of a canonical text.

When reflecting on their curriculum orientations, teachers might also affirm their commitment to teaching concrete, particularized skills, as is prioritized in a "scientific" orientation to curriculum (Bobbitt, 1918/2009). Advocates of this approach to curriculum argue that students' learning should be understood as involving discrete behaviors that can be methodically taught. This orientation might be pursued during a civic literacy project if the teacher seeks to foster a series of particular cognitive skills as the students comprehend and compose texts on civic issues.

For example, during the phase of problem exploration, students will likely be reading a variety of print texts. Reading comprehension is arguably bolstered when students know how to perform the cognitive skills of summarizing, predicting, questioning, and clarifying areas of texts that are unclear (Schoenbach et al., 1999). Each of these skills can be modeled and then practiced in a methodological fashion *while* students are reading texts on relevant civic issues.

Given this potential for a layering of curriculum orientations, teachers can begin the unit design process by identifying their own orientation and overall motivations to teach. Assuming that teachers interested in civic literacy projects are drawn to the social reconstructionist orientation, they can first reflect on this orientation and confirm the importance of teaching for social change and civic engagement. Then, to stimulate their reflection on the role of other orientations in their teaching, teachers can pursue additional questions:

- What other values guide my practice as a teacher? For example, in what ways do I want to integrate canonical knowledge? Develop students' individualized interests? Build students' particularized cognitive skills?
- How have I experienced various curriculum orientations in my own schooling, and how do these experiences compare to what I wish to scaffold for my students?
- How have my own life experiences outside of school informed my views of schooling and my curriculum orientations?

I offer one cautionary note on this reflection: While certain curriculum orientations do not have to be enacted to the exclusion of others, some orientations interrupt or drain power from others. For example, a social reconstructionist curriculum orientation might be hampered if a teacher feels strongly that academic core knowledge, or canonical knowledge, plays a central role in the classroom. Indeed, when teaching for core knowledge, teachers often teach for coverage—so that particular pieces of knowledge or texts are understood and consumed by the students, without a strong focus on questioning and critical exploration. This approach can position students as passive recipients of knowledge. In comparison, civic literacy projects, and the social reconstructionist orientation overall, ask students to be active creators of knowledge that will enable them to make change in the world. Therefore, a core-knowledge approach should only be integrated in ways that preserve the potential for students to question texts and act on their insights. Aspects of various orientations can be drawn on simultaneously, but teachers should make sure that their orientation frames students as critical agents, able to examine and address relevant social problems.

ESTABLISH A LONG-TERM FRAMEWORK

Moving from the theoretical work of establishing curriculum orientations to the more time-bound, unit-specific work of setting goals and designing assignments, unit design often begins when teachers develop a long-term vision of what should happen by the end of the unit. This helps teachers ensure that lessons are strategically enacted and build up to a clear culminating point. Below I describe a number of resources that can help educators think long-term about their units.

Standards

When engaging in long-term curriculum planning, teachers commonly look to local, state, or national standards that outline what students should be doing in particular content areas and often in reference to particular grades. Some teachers independently study standards and choose which standards to address in which unit. Other teachers work in teams to identify a curriculum pacing calendar that sets out how they will address the standards throughout the year. Given these and other situations, unit design for civic literacy projects is often well-aided by attention to indicators set out in various standards.

A reminder and caveat before continuing: Given the current emphasis on and pressure to cover standards, particularly the Common Core State Standards (CCSS) (National Governors Association Center for Best Practices, Council of Chief State School Officers, 2010), teachers might be inclined to organize their curriculum so that they move from standard to standard, tackling one at a time, with less regard for the material actually being discussed. Instead, teachers should prioritize meaningful issues and activities that thus address standards (Beach et al., 2012). As introduced in Chapter 1, this approach places priority on building units around relevant topics as opposed to only prioritizing thinking about how the units meet the standards. Yet it acknowledges how units on such relevant topics can unfold in meaningful ways when the standards are met.

Imagine a 9th-grade humanities teacher who is committed to a social reconstructionist curriculum orientation and seeks to enact a civic literacy project at some point during the school year. This teacher decides to draw from content-area specific standards as presented by the National Council of Teachers of English (NCTE) and the International Reading Association (IRA) (2009) to help her with her planning. Standard 7, which calls on students to "conduct research on issues and interests by generating ideas and questions, and by posing problems," fits perfectly, as she definitely intends on having students read and question the views in various informational, nonfiction texts on socially important topics. Specifically, many students in her class are motivated by questions about healthcare reform, and the teacher is planning a series of lessons where students will read op-eds that articulate diverse views on what kind of healthcare policies are most needed in the United States. In line with the standard, which requires that students compose "questions" and pose "problems," she will require students to raise questions about the authors' intents and point out possible drawbacks to their arguments. She also plans on consulting NCTE and IRA standards on writing and speaking/listening and designing standards-based activities in these modalities to further explore the issue of healthcare reform.

A separate group of 9th-grade teachers looks to the CCSS and maps particular standards from this document to the civic literacy project they are envisioning. They plan to select novels that portray social problems and organize the students in literature circles where each circle reads a different novel. Given this vision, two Common Core reading standards jump out as appropriate: "Determine a theme or central idea of a text and analyze in detail its development over the course of the text, including how it emerges and is shaped and refined by specific details" (Reading Standard #2, Grades 9–10) and "Analyze how complex characters (e.g., those with multiple or conflicting motivations) develop over the course of a text, interact with other characters, and advance the plot or develop the theme" (Reading Standard #3, Grades 9–10). To meet these standards, the teachers design assignments that ask students to identify the central political idea in their assigned text, or what messages the text sends about a social problem, and analyze how the characters relate to the social problem and take action, or not, over the course of the text. These examples illustrate how standards can influence teachers' visions of what students do during a civic literacy project.

Long-Term Objectives

Long-term planning also involves teachers identifying unit-long objectives, or statements that illustrate the teachers' and students' goals for the unit. These objectives are ideally based on what a teacher has already learned about the students' skills and knowledge and illustrate how he or she will advance their learning from its current place. Objectives are generally written in statement form, beginning with phrasing such as "Students will be able to . . ." So, if the central civic problem is our depleting energy sources, some long-term objectives might include the following:

- Students will be able to understand the multiple causes and effects of unstable sources of energy.
- Students will be able to compare various present-day approaches to solving the energy problem.
- Students will be able to advocate for a solution to the energy problem.

These objectives imply three key phases of the project: The students will first understand different facets of the problem, then study competing approaches to the problem, and ultimately, take action to advocate for a particular way to address it. The objectives further imply that based on prior assessments, the teacher believes the students will benefit as they develop such knowledge about the energy problem and the skills of cause–effect analysis, comparison, and advocacy.

Note that the objectives leave aspects of how the unit will unfold undetermined. Specifically, they do not confirm what approaches to the energy problem will be studied, what approaches the students will advocate for, or what particular action steps the students will take when they advocate for a solution. These elements can be determined with the students, based on their interests and research. For example, through research, students might learn of a letter-writing campaign being organized by a community-based organization in regard to energy use and decide to participate in it. In this case, the final objective about advocacy could be revised to read, "Students will be able to advocate for a solution to the energy problem through a letter-writing campaign."

Many civic literacy projects do not begin with an identified problem; the students and teacher plan to choose a problem on which to focus after studying various local, national, and global issues. In these cases, a teacher might ask the students to write persuasive pieces arguing why the class should take up particular issues, allowing the students' voices to meaningfully inform the project. Accordingly, one objective of the unit could be "Students will be able to write proposals outlining the importance of addressing selected civic issues." Such an objective formalizes the expectation that the students will search out various possible problems to address during the problem identification phase of the project, choose one that they think holds the most importance for their project, and then justify their choice in writing. The students would then study and take action on the problem or problems that they selected through this process.

Just as students' voices and interests can be represented in the unit objectives, unit objectives also often signify what resources will anchor the unit. Civic literacy projects productively involve varied resources including newspapers, videos, and poetry (see Chapter 3 for a review of eight different types of resources), and these resources can be referenced in the objectives, signifying their centrality to the unit. For example, a teacher might read *Fast Food Nation: The Dark Side of the All-American Meal* (Schlosser, 2001) and decide that segments of the text should be placed at the heart of a unit on the fast-food industry. This teacher would then compose objectives for a unit that would ask students to analyze the text's central ideas, evaluate the author's use of evidence, and write their own argumentative texts on the industry.

Other teachers might first compose general objectives for the unit and then find resources that will help them meet the goals. For example, if a unit includes the objective that "Students will be able to deliberate on the benefits and drawbacks to various approaches to immigration reform," the teacher will need to seek out resources that portray three to four such approaches. Whether resources are selected in response to the objectives or the objectives are written with the assumption that certain preselected resources will be used, resources should help the students pursue larger goals set out in the long-term framework (Wiggins & McTighe, 2005). Clear objectives give teachers and students a guiding light as they begin to think about what they want to study and how they want to take action during the civic literacy project.

Paving the Road for Inquiry

In addition to objectives, open-ended questions also guide students' inquiries throughout a unit. These might be called "essential questions" as they are the questions that are essential to, or at the heart of, the study (Jacobs, 1997; Wiggins & McTighe, 2005). Sometimes teachers rewrite the long-term objectives so that they are worded as questions, as a means of determining the unit's key overarching questions (Blythe & Associates, 1998). Drawing on the example above, a unit objective of "Students will be able to compare various present-day approaches to solving the energy problem" could be rewritten as "What different approaches are individuals and policymakers taking to solve the energy problem, and how do they compare?"

Essential questions ignite student curiosity and signify to students that the teacher hopes to learn and inquire with them as opposed to assuming that they will arrive at preset answers (Jacobs, 1997). Illustrating the value of essential questions, Jacobs offers many sets of questions to utilize in different grade levels. For example, she proposes these essential questions for a unit on AIDS:

- What is AIDS, and how is it different from other viruses?
- How does AIDS affect the individual?
- How does AIDS affect society?
- What can I do to prevent the spread of AIDS? (p. 67)

These are suggested for a middle school, 2-week, schoolwide unit enacted across disciplines. They stand as a worthy model of essential questions for civic literacy projects because they imply that the students will both explore the contextual impact of AIDS and take action.

Similarly, *Understanding Fiscal Responsibility (UFR): A Curriculum for Teaching About the Federal Budget, National Debt, and Budget Deficit* (2012) opens with an invitation for teachers and students to answer key questions:

- What do the decisions we make about the federal budget, national debt, and budget deficit say about who we are as people?
- How should we address our nation's fiscal challenges now and in the future to assure that our decisions are consistent with our values and traditions?

Intended for high school economics, civics/government, history, or mathematics classrooms, these questions lend focus to the students' work on the issue of U.S. fiscal challenges.

When drafting essential questions in the beginning stages of unit planning, it is recommended that teachers compose two to five essential questions (Jacobs, 1997; Wiggins & McTighe, 2005), perhaps mirroring two to five long-term objectives. Keeping student engagement at the forefront, the questions should reflect the students' interests about particular social problems and possibly be drafted collaboratively with them. The questions outline the scope and sequence of the unit so that, in reading them, any outside observer could understand the different topics or inquiries the students will be taking up and the order in which they will be addressed. Most importantly, essential questions are most effective when they can only be debated through ongoing inquiry and cannot be answered with a simple "yes" or "no." Essential questions are difficult to ever stop answering—they have so many answers that can constantly be uncovered. Through this process of discovery, the students develop deep understandings of the central topic. As a result, when applied to civic literacy projects, they motivate students to pursue long-term investigations about civic problems.

Alongside the essential questions, when establishing a long-term framework, teachers can compose "enduring understandings," or meaningful understandings about the problem at hand (Wiggins & McTighe, 2005). Enduring understandings begin with the phrase "Students will understand that . . ." and outline what the teacher hopes the students will understand over the course of the unit. In the case of a unit on the federal budget, teachers might compose the following enduring understandings:

- Students will understand that the challenges regarding national budgets are complex and solutions will require trade-offs.
- Students will understand that current challenges are framed by historical events, including the creation of Social Security and Medicare.

In comparison to essential questions, such understandings are primarily of use to the teacher, as "the point is to clearly frame our goals for ourselves (and colleagues)," and if posted for the students, it might suggest that they are to recite these statements to show understanding (Wiggins & McTighe, 2005, p. 141). Instead, the teacher can keep a record of some proposed understandings in his or her own notes and then craft instruction that moves students towards them, adjusting the enduring understandings over time if students' studies take them on a different path.

DESIGN KEY PERFORMANCE TASKS

After reflecting on a curriculum orientation and establishing a long-term framework, a next step for teachers is to think more concretely about what they want students to *do* to meet the objectives and answer the essential questions. In this process, teachers compose ideas of performance tasks, or assignments, yielding oral, visual, and print-based products that can illustrate the students' growing civic understandings. For example, students might collect photographs and newspaper articles in a "social problem scrapbook" and then, surrounding these artifacts, write analytic annotations about the genesis and possible amelioration of the problems portrayed. Pursuing this performance task could help them meet the long-term objective of "Students will be able to analyze visual and print informational texts portraying social problems." This is one example of a performance task, or project-based assignment, that students could work on in a civic literacy project.

While the culture of schooling often assumes that teachers assess student learning by scheduling tests, tests cannot illustrate students' abilities to use their knowledge in authentic ways. Test questions are predetermined, and students have to answer them within a prescribed medium, usually within a limited period of time. In comparison, students pursue project-based assignments over time, and they can ultimately illustrate a varied set of authentic and democratically productive skills such as deliberation and collaboration. Therefore, project-based assignments, or performance tasks, are key for civic literacy projects, as these tasks involve the types of reading, speaking, and writing skills that activists pursue outside of the classroom.

Furthermore, students should have opportunities to work towards goals that reflect their interests and/or needs, and in pursuing a performance task as opposed to the whole class completing one uniform test, this type of learning is afforded. For example, students who are skilled in creating digital videos might compose a digital text documenting a particular social problem, while students who are skilled writers can compose an accompanying, explanatory review of the video. Or, teachers can ask students who struggle in writing to take up the challenge of writing the review with the support of their peers, while students who struggle with video-making can be asked to develop their skills in this area. Performance tasks can allow for this differentiated instruction and for students to work on different levels and skills.

Given their importance, I argue that performance tasks form the backbone of civic literacy projects. Students can pursue introductory performances at the start of the project, guided inquiry performances through the middle of the project, and culminating performances at the end of the project (Blythe & Associates, 1998). I explore the roles of such performance tasks in civic literacy projects below.

Introductory Performance

In civic literacy projects, introductory performances are ripe opportunities for students to consider a wide range of social problems, exploring their prior knowledge and interests, with the goal of ultimately choosing one or some problems to focus on for the remainder of the project. In these scenarios, it is quite generative for the teacher and/or students to facilitate a class-wide open forum where students air the problems that face the school or community. Such a forum led to the safe sex health fair run by and for 9th-graders and is a natural starting point for civic literacy projects.

First, in preparation for, or in the context of, a forum dedicated to brainstorming social problems, students might complete autobiographical, personal narratives on how particular civic problems impact their own lives. Or students and their teacher can take a tour of the community, capturing pictures with disposable or digital cameras of scenes or moments that represent social problems. In their notebooks, students can write reflectively about their observations, responding to prompts such as:

- During our community walk, I was concerned to see . . .
- I was surprised that . . .
- I expected to see . . .
- I think it is important for our class to do something about . . .

See Teacher Resource A for a sample worksheet. Free printable PDF versions of all Teacher Resources are available for download at tcpress.com.

Second, teachers can open the forums by asking, "What bothers you? What problems do you see in your community?" and record students' answers on the board. During the forum, students should reference their autobiographical writing, photographs, and/or notes from the community walk. Ideally, they will have collected all of these materials in a folder dedicated to the civic literacy project which they will add to over the course of the unit. Third, students can sign up to do follow-up research on one of the listed problems to learn about current advocacy campaigns and policy ideas individuals and groups have proposed to address the problem. Through these introductory performances, students work as ethnographers and concerned citizens studying their community.

In other cases, the teacher and/or students know of a pressing social problem that is automatically centered as their topic of focus. For example, imagine if weeks before a teacher planned to begin a civic literacy project, a new security company began working in the school, scanning students' backpacks and frisking random students looking for weapons. Prior to the hiring of the new company, these things had not been done. During these weeks, the new policing policies became a topic of constant conversation

Teacher Resource A—Community Walk Reflection Sheet

This past week, we walked on the blocks surrounding our school, observing and taking notes on social problems in our community. Use the space below to reflect on what you saw.

During our community walk, I was concerned to see . . .

_____

_____

_____

_____

I was surprised that . . .

_____

_____

_____

I expected to see . . .

_____

_____

_____

I think it is important for our class to do something about . . . (name no more than 2 issues)

_____

_____

_____

both during class time and in the hallways. Given this, the teacher plans to propose to the students that they focus their civic project on the topic of school security. If a particular issue is an obvious choice, as in this scenario, the introductory performance task could be framed not as an open forum on multiple issues, but as a means to gather students' views on that particular issue. The students' responses would help the teacher assess the students' viewpoints on how the problem should be addressed.

If the teacher can predict that there will be many contested views on how to approach an issue within the class, a performance task could ask students to briefly consider varying standpoints, as articulated in classroom discussion or in the media, and share their initial opinions on them. For example, a teacher can enact a four-corners exercise where he writes four different viewpoints on an issue and asks students to sit down next to the sign that best represents their opinion and discuss it with their classmates. Or teachers might distribute opinionnaires, documents that present students with provocative statements on the topic at hand and ask them to mark each statement with an A (for agree) or a D (for disagree) and to explain their thinking (Wilhelm, 2007).

Consider a case where a teacher distributes an opinionnaire on marriage equality, a topic that the teacher decides to frame as controversial, given recent public debates about it (Hess, 2009a). A survey prompts high school students to respond to statements including the following:

- Marriage is between a man and a woman.
- All consenting adults have the right to get married.
- The government should create policy that regulates marriage.

See Teacher Resource B for a sample worksheet. Like this example, opinionnaires should present ranges of opinions that exist within our cultural landscape and introduce arguments that students will encounter as they engage in the problem exploration phase. As they react to the arguments, the worksheet asks students to share their own views on the statements, illustrating how they should not simply and exclusively adopt or reject the preprepared statements without explaining themselves.

As suggested in the examples above, it may often be the case that the introductory performance task asks the students to engage in problem identification, or the first steps of problem exploration, yet an opening performance task could also be an action step. For example, a school might be organizing an evening where students serve food at a homeless shelter. This could be framed as the introductory performance task where students provide an immediate service to the community by working at the shelter and, as a result, are exposed to the dilemma of homelessness in their city. Then, such service-learning is extended as teachers ask students to engage in an

Teacher Resource B—What's Your Opinion?

You have shown interest in studying the topic of marriage equality. There is much public conversation about this topic. Judges in our courts and legislators in our government have weighed in, making important rulings about who can get married to whom.

In this activity, you will reflect on your own opinions on marriage. Next to each statement, circle Agree or Disagree. Underneath each statement, write a sentence explaining your reaction to the statement.

Marriage is between a man and a woman.   **Agree Disagree**

_____

_____

The government should create policy
that regulates marriage.   **Agree Disagree**

_____

_____

All consenting adults have the right to get married.   **Agree Disagree**

_____

_____

People get married so that they can have children.   **Agree Disagree**

_____

_____

It is good for society when consenting
adults get married.   **Agree Disagree**

_____

_____

open forum, autobiographical writing, or opinionnaires to more sharply name and explore the problem at hand—in this case homelessness.

In summary, possible introductory performance tasks include the following:

- Open forum
- Personal narrative
- Community walk (coupled with photography and reflective writing)
- Small-group discussion
- Opinionnaire
- Service-learning project

Guided Inquiry Performance

Guided inquiry performances are the tasks that ask students to dig into the social problem they are addressing, learning about its nuances and questioning their initial assumptions, as aired through their introductory performances. In a civic literacy project, this is where the problem exploration is likely to occur. During problem exploration, teachers and students explore how a problem manifests itself, how it has taken shape at different points in history, and multiple stances on how it could be addressed. Specifically, they read various texts and write, draw, act, and talk so as to make sense of and document their emerging findings. The students' guided inquiry work can illustrate their interests, struggles, questions, and developing skills for their teachers, who can then plan subsequent instruction based on their assessment of student learning.

In that teachers use guided inquiry performances as a means to determine how students' knowledge about social problems is developing, the performances are the means through which the students display their knowledge and skill. Thus, a guided inquiry performance could be the keeping of a media analysis portfolio that tracks how different periodicals are reporting on the students' issue. Here, students collect artifacts, such as newspaper articles, and then reflect in writing on what these artifacts say about their identified problem.

Some teachers ask students to write freely in their journals or portfolios about their developing civic insights. For example, when studying proposed budget cuts to a local park, 7th-graders read numerous newspaper articles on the state budget deficit and recorded "jottings" as instructed during their English language arts period. Students independently chose which details to record and reflect on in their journals, as the assignment was rather open-ended. The students had previously used this strategy during their independent reading activities and now applied it to their reading of informational, nonfiction texts on the state budget. The race awareness after-school program facilitators also asked students to share open-ended, individualized reactions to texts, but instead of writing in private journals, the students wrote on large sheets of poster paper hung for all to see.

In other classrooms, teachers expect students to respond to multiple predetermined prompts or a graphic organizer that elicits particular details about each of their readings on social problems. In these cases, the writing tasks are structured with more teacher direction and are less free-form. For example, for each text that the student reads, he or she might be asked to share three new vocabulary words, two key quotes, and a sentence on the author's purpose. The authors' purposes might be to advocate for a particular viewpoint, to summarize the conflicting viewpoints shared by the public, or to share a personal anecdote about how the problem is experienced by an individual. See Teacher Resource C on the next page for a sample graphic organizer that prompts students to record particular details about news media. Before asking the students to complete such an organizer on their own, the teacher can model how it is used with a newspaper article she has selected. Whether implemented with more or less structure, guided inquiry tasks ask students to record their developing knowledge about an identified social problem.

Guided inquiry is productively pursued in small groups. In a minimally structured scenario, students arrive to class having read a common text the day before or having interviewed a family member on a topic (e.g., immigration, U.S. military actions) and then work in small groups to discuss their reactions. One student should be assigned the role of note-taker, responsible for recording the group's most valuable insights. Alternatively, the experience can be organized with more structure where each student is assigned a particular role for the discussion. For example, students can assume the following roles:

- One student is required to keep the discussion focused.
- One student is responsible for recording key terms that are used in the article and in the discussion.
- One student is responsible for writing questions that come up about the problem.

The students might also be required to answer predetermined focus questions during their small-group meetings.

To consider a small-group assignment that involves deliberation, imagine teams of three to four students who are addressing the problem of mass shootings in the United States. First they spend 3 days reading and taking notes on an issue advisory pamphlet entitled *How Can We Stop Mass Shootings in Our Communities?* (National Issues Forums Institute, 2013). It

Teacher Resource C—Reading and Reflection on the Media

This week, you will research how your group's chosen issue has been covered in the media. Over the course of the week, take the following steps:

1. Visit the following newspapers' websites: *The New York Times*, *The Wall Street Journal*, *The Guardian*, and a local news source.

2. In the search engine on each site, insert the search terms related to your chosen issue that your group determined.

3. When you find a related news article, print it and bring it to your desk.

4. As you read the article, underline sentences that you think are important and that will help you complete the chart below.

5. Fill in the following chart for each article.

Title	
Author	
Newspaper and Date	
Key Quote from Article	
Key Quote from Article	
Author's Purpose for Writing the Article	
Key Words, Names, Terms (list at least 3)	

reviews three possible responses to this question, proposing policy measures that (1) restrict the availability of dangerous weapons, (2) equip people to defend themselves, and (3) root out violence in our culture (e.g., video-games). Then, the students work in small groups to answer the following questions, in regard to each possible response:

- Who benefits from this choice?
- What are the drawbacks of this choice?
- What must be done to implement this choice? (*Teacher's Guide to National Issues Forums [NIF] in the Classroom*, 2001, p. 3.45).

After talking for 15 minutes, the students individually write their answers on preprepared worksheets and, in turn, address the objective of analyzing various viewpoints on the issue of gun control. The next day, the teacher facilitates a whole-class deliberative forum where the students voice their views and explore what stances they will advocate for during this civic literacy project.

Finally, the phase of guided inquiry can be used as a site for students to question how to move beyond charity-oriented service-learning. In the section above, I posed the possibility of students' working in a homeless shelter as their introductory performance. Say this action step was to continue throughout the civic literacy project, with the students making weekly trips to the shelter and keeping a journal or engaging in small-group discussions following each visit as a guided inquiry performance task. In their writing or discussion, students can be required to consider the possibility of policy-oriented approaches to improving the lives of homeless citizens, as many shelter-based services only represent short-term measures. See Teacher Resource D on the next page for prompts to aid in this process in regards to a number of different service projects. Given the amount of time they have spent in the shelter, students may be able to share personal stories that illustrate the ways in which the needs of the individuals at the shelter are not being fully met through food distribution. This can lead them to propose ways that they can contribute to greater change for homeless citizens through public advocacy.

To review, as students are learning about their identified social problem through guided inquiry, teachers can assign the following performance tasks to support and assess their learning:

- Journal writing/note-taking
- Artifact collection with accompanying student reflections
- Small-group discussions
- Community interviews
- Deliberative forums

Teacher Resource D—Moving Towards Action

You have spent many hours offering your services to individuals in need at different sites in our town. Some of you have worked in hospitals, some of you have worked in homeless shelters, and some of you in an early-childhood day care center. Answer the questions below so as to reflect on your experience and consider how the lives of the individuals you served may be improved.

1. What are the key needs of the individuals at your site? Name at least 2.

2. How have you helped the people at your site?

3. Think of at least 1 instance where you could **not** provide the help that you felt was needed by someone, or many people, at the site. Describe what happened.

4. Given what you described in No. 3, what would help this person or people? Would it help if the site had more funding from the government? Would it help if the staff had different training? Would it help if there were fewer people being serviced at this site? Would it help if anything else about the site was different? Would it help if the people's experiences outside of the site (e.g., in their homes, streets, and schools) were different? You can respond to any of these questions or propose another suggestion.

5. Who do you think we should talk with to learn more about how to improve the lives of the people at your site?

Culminating Performance

The culminating performances are tasks that come at the end of the unit and ask students to present their final analyses of the social problem, make use of all that they have studied, and prove their ability to meet some of the long-term objectives of the unit. A culminating performance is the "final project"—the research report, oral presentation, school play, or some other concluding assignment that asks students to draw on what they learned while pursuing the introductory and guided inquiry performances (Blythe & Associates, 1998). Often, the culminating performance is the action step of a civic literacy project, as it is at the close of the project that students best understand their problem and know the message that they want to get out to the public. In this case, the culminating performance can be a task where students compose print, oral, and/or visual texts to deliver to public audiences. To this end, once the introductory and guided inquiry performance tasks are complete, teachers plan additional forums, or discussions, where students decide what type of texts they want to create so as to bring their messages for social change out of the classroom.

Considering possible written products, students might compose opinion pieces or persuasive letters for their culminating performances. To scaffold instruction as students compose persuasive letters, teachers can ensure that students first deliberate on various stances to their chosen issue during the guided inquiry performance. Then, once they are armed with a firm opinion, they are ready to outline and draft a letter that documents their knowledge about the issue and informs their audience about how to act on or think about a problem, such as how they should vote (*Teacher's Guide to National Issues Forums [NIF] in the Classroom*, 2001). For example, the 7th-graders in the park project wrote persuasive letters to their local assemblyperson telling him to vote against the park budget cuts and offering suggestions of ways to bring money to the park budget—suggestions which they had explored in class.

When writing persuasive texts, teachers support students to include an acknowledgment of their opponents' views and responses to those views. For example, if the students are writing to their city's mayor to argue that their city needs stronger gun-control laws, after supporting their argument with specific reasoning, they can acknowledge the arguments of those who think that such gun-control measures are unnecessary and talk back to them. See Teacher Resource E on the next page for a template fostering this process.

To build their understanding of these counterarguments, teachers can stage mini-debates as students are writing their culminating persuasive texts. According to one model, students are assigned opposing sides of an argument (e.g., pro and against gun control) and then engage in small-group debate by using preprepared notes (Felton & Herko, 2004). Following the debate, they take more notes on how they might have better responded to the criticism

_____
Teacher Resource E—Crafting a Persuasive Letter
_____

You have spent weeks studying gun control and believe that individuals should have limited access to guns. During the open forum last week, you decided to try to convince our city's mayor to push for stricter gun-control measures for the state. Presently, the state has weak gun-control laws. You will communicate to him about this by writing him a persuasive letter. We will also try to set up a meeting with one of his staff members.

Use this organizer below to brainstorm ideas for your letter. The key argument has already been filled in.

Argument—Individuals should have limited access to guns, and state legislation should be passed that ensures this.
Reasons and Explanation of Argument—Make brief notes about 3 points that support your argument. Reference the ideas from our class readings:
Criticism—Acknowledge at least 2 points that those against gun control might say to criticize your reasoning:
Response—Explain how you would respond to these criticisms:

This graphic organizer draws from the ideas presented in Felton, M. K., & Herko, S. (2004). From dialogue to two-sided argument: Scaffolding adolescents' persuasive writing. *Journal of Adolescent and Adult Literacy, 47*(8), 672–683.

they received from their opponent and convinced him/her of their key point. Finally, they use these notes when drafting and revising their persuasive texts.

Persuasive writing is powerfully supported by visual images that illustrate the students' central argument, or a persuasive text could be entirely composed of visual images if students design murals, create films, or organize photographs so as to argue a particular point. Students may compose digital videos that communicate clear civic messages and distribute them to multiple audiences over the Internet. When teachers and students pursue this type of performance task, they exercise skills in digital technology.

The culminating performance could also advance students' oral literacy skills. A public deliberative forum could be framed as the culminating performance where the teacher assesses students' abilities to acknowledge and counter varying points of view on the issue, or students might lead a schoolwide deliberation on the topic at hand, again, if the goal is to explore opinions.

If the goal of the culminating performance is not to have students talk about varying opinions (assuming this was done as a guided inquiry performance), but instead to put forward a cohesive, persuasive opinion through oral text, then the culminating task could involve students organizing an assembly or play in which they share their view on the issue, or many issues, and advocate for particular forms of social change. This is what occurred in the social justice writing assignment, as the students read speeches, delivered PowerPoint presentations with accompanying photographs, and recited poems in an end-of-the-year assembly. In another case, elementary students who tackled the problem of child labor performed a play that addressed the plight of child laborers in the past and today for their culminating performance (Rogovin, 1998). They also wrote letters to manufacturers about their use of child labor.

While most of the above examples equate the culminating performance with the civic action step, a valuable culminating performance could be a writing assignment where students reflect on the strengths and limitations of their work. In this case, teachers support students to analyze whom they did and did not impact and what next steps they will take as activists. Teachers can frame this analysis and reflection as the key culminating event of the project if the students took action in regard to their issue in prior weeks.

To review, possible culminating performance tasks for civic literacy projects include the following:

- Persuasive letters
- Digital videos
- Deliberative forums
- Public presentations
- School play
- Reflective papers assessing the civic literacy project

Creating and Using Criteria

Crafting performances also involves crafting criteria that describe the markers of excellence for the performances. The criteria aid the teacher and the students as they assess their work and give feedback. For a short assignment, perhaps an introductory performance, the criteria and the feedback might be relatively informal. For example, students might simply receive a check, a check plus, or a check minus on notebook entries based on the two expectations that they (1) include observations of a social problem in their neighborhood and (2) include descriptive language. For a performance on which students will be spending multiple days or weeks, or that counts for a large portion of their grade, it is likely that the criteria will be more detailed, the teacher will spend more time reviewing the performance, and feedback will be more extensive.

The criteria should list clearly and plainly what should be exhibited in the students' work. For example, a criteria sheet for an assignment entitled "Essay with an Attitude" is based on the following headings: "thesis; introduction; evidence; conclusion; tight writing; grammar, punctuation, spelling checked and corrected" (Christensen, 2000, p. 79). The sheet prompts the students to ensure that their essays contain all of these sections, which are briefly defined. The assignment asks them to write persuasive essays in which they state their opinions on contemporary issues, and in order to show proficiency in this task—one that might play a prominent role in a civic literacy project—the students work to meet the defined set of criteria.

In comparison to a single list of criteria, teachers and/or students can also construct multiple sets of descriptors outlining what is included in outstanding, fair, and poor versions of the product. The options are presented as a chart, often called a rubric, with one column listing the qualities of an outstanding product, another listing the qualities of a fair product, and the final column listing the qualities of an emerging product in need of major revision. Some teachers choose to avoid rubrics, at least at the start of the project, because they appear too cumbersome and can overwhelm the students. However, once students have a rough draft, written with the aid of a list of criteria of what should be included in an outstanding product, they might be ready to think about their work in a more complex way. A rubric can help them question whether they have completed each necessary element in an outstanding, mediocre, or incomplete manner.

Whether presenting a singular list of criteria or a rubric showing multiple levels, students can help determine the assessment criteria. Specifically, students can analyze different products and discuss what makes them outstanding, fair, or poor. The teacher can then generalize the issues they raise in their analysis and insert them into the rubrics or criteria sheets. This helps students know what they should do when composing their own products.

For example, picture a class of students analyzing a digital video, up-loaded onto the Internet by a teenager in another city, documenting how and why youth in their neighborhood suffer from asthma. After watching the video, the students conclude that one reason why the video is good is because the footage sharply illustrates the frustration and pain asthmatics experience. They are moved by the way the video reveals these real-life experiences of people living with asthma. Given this, the teacher writes in the rubric that "video footage should be accurate and revealing." The process then continues as the students identify a series of qualities of the video and they are recorded on the rubric to guide the students' creation of their own videos.

Criteria are best used if they guide an ongoing assessment process that prioritizes formative assessment (Blythe & Associates, 1998; Wiggins & McTighe, 2005). In this process, students receive feedback, based on pub-licly shared understandings of what is expected, so as to improve their work and guide their learning as they move forward. The students should receive this feedback before the final product is submitted or delivered and evalu-ated. To illustrate, before their social action assembly, Scott Rosner—the teacher leading the project—gave feedback to the students who would be presenting their work. Margaret, who prepared a PowerPoint presentation about trash collection in her neighborhood, originally planned to read the text on each slide. Then, through formative feedback, Scott reminded her of the expectation that the oral text be somewhat different from the print text in the PowerPoint and asked her to consider that all of the posted text need not be read aloud. At the end of their conversation, Margaret went to find a highlighter to highlight the select parts of the PowerPoint that she would read aloud. This illustrates how brief conversations based on previously re-viewed criteria can help students improve their work. Teachers might share feedback during a teacher–student conference or by writing comments on a draft of student work. Teachers might also check off items on a criteria sheet, signifying the criteria the student is meeting, and circle the items the student needs to improve.

Students can also give each other feedback, through a peer-assessment process, and engage in self-assessment by reviewing their work and then writ-ing or speaking with a peer about what criteria they are and are not meeting. Imagine that students are working on small-group oral presentations on their stances on the U.S. role in a current international conflict. They will ultimate-ly share their presentations with the class as a guided inquiry performance task intended to develop students' knowledge about the conflict. Earlier in the week, the groups finalized the scripts for their presentations and designed posters and/or PowerPoint presentations to display. They arrived to class today knowing that they would receive feedback on their presentations from one other group and suggestions for how to improve them.

The peer-assessment activity opens with the teacher asking each group to write down two or three concerns they have about their presentations, in reference to previously presented criteria. The criteria are as follows:

- All students speak during the group presentation.
- Students speak clearly with good intonation, making eye contact with the audience.
- Students use visual and media displays to enhance the presentation.
- Students articulate one succinct, overarching opinion about the conflict.
- Students make at least three substantive points that draw from our class readings and support the overarching message.
- Students share at least two next steps that they believe the government should take in reference to the conflict.

Then, each group goes to sit with another group in a particular corner of the room. In these corners, first, the presenting group shares its concerns and then rehearses its presentation to the other group that is responsible for recording its feedback on a peer-assessment sheet. Second, the assessing group shares its feedback with the presenters on how well they met the criteria for the presentations and on ways to address the group's stated concerns. Finally, in discussion with the presenters, the assessors write down at least three "next steps" the presenters will take to improve their presentations. At the conclusion of this process, the roles reverse, and the assessing group becomes the presenting group. See Teacher Resource F on pages 136–137 for a peer-editing sheet that presents these criteria as well as space for the peer assessors to insert their comments and record next steps.

Importantly, as teachers and students identify their areas of strength and need, whole-class or small-group instruction should be based around the areas in need of improvement. For example, given that the above assignment asks the students to articulate a clear opinion on an international conflict, if a select set of students does not articulate a clear opinion in their rehearsal performance, the teacher could meet with those students and share some options of potential opinions and ask them to choose one that most reflects their views. It is through such instruction that students can improve their work. In civic literacy projects, as student work improves, student voices shine and articulate important messages for social change. Clear criteria, outlining what is entailed in excellent work, and instruction that helps students meet the criteria enable this form of participation and learning.

CRAFT A PLAN FOR LEARNING

In the final part of the curriculum design process—crafting a plan for learning—teachers and students think in a more concrete, day-to-day way about how the unit will unfold. The plan for learning should relate to the long-term framework and the key performance tasks, as daily lesson plans and activities should help students meet long-term objectives and create outstanding performance tasks. While aspects of a civic literacy project can evolve as it is pursued and long-term objectives might sharpen or change, daily lessons should be of service to larger goals.

It is helpful to hold in mind two key questions so as to align day-to-day learning with a long-term plan. In order for the students to successfully meet the long-term objectives, answer the essential questions, and meet the criteria for the performance tasks, teachers can ask (1) "How much time should be allocated for the different performances, and how can these performances be plotted on a unit timeline?" and (2) "How will the lesson plans support student achievement in regard to the long-term framework and performances?" I discuss the processes of composing timelines and lessons below.

Composing a Timeline

When composing timelines, teachers consider how they want to order their performance tasks and how much time they think they should allot to each one. A timeline might take the shape of a calendar, similar to what is seen in many teacher planning guides. Or a timeline might be written as an outline where activities for "Week 1," "Week 2," and so on are listed in a linear format, similar to what is seen in many college syllabi. Then, in each box of the calendar, or on each line of the outline, the teacher writes a short description of what will happen on that day. When teaching a class in curriculum development, I require preservice teachers to create timelines when designing units, and it is often with this activity that they are able to get the most concrete vision of how their instruction will unfold. Indeed, after they make their timelines, many revise their long-term objectives and add or delete performance tasks that they see no longer fit. This same process should help sharpen civic literacy projects. See Teacher Resource G on pages 138–139 for a sample timeline of a unit involving a civic literacy project. This unit timeline does not explicitly reference any particular social issue or resources to be used to study the issue. Instead, it shows how multiple weeks of sequenced instruction can be used to scaffold civic literacy projects in general.

Teacher Resource F—Oral Presentation Peer-Assessment Form

You have been working in small groups to create an oral presentation on U.S. involvement in the wars in Iraq, Afghanistan, or Syria. This week, every small group in the class will present its oral presentation to another group. Use this worksheet to assess the presentation that you will watch.

Concerns: First, ask the presenting group what concerns and questions it has about its presentation and write them below.

1. _____

   _____

2. _____

   _____

Assessment: Second, while you are watching the group's presentation, take notes on the following chart. Assuming you will not be able to finish the whole chart during the group's presentation, take some time after the presentation to complete it. Keep in mind the concerns that the group members shared. You will later submit your notes to the group members and they will use your feedback to improve their work.

Criteria	Your feedback
All students speak during the group presentation	Circle one: Yes / No
Students speak clearly with good intonation, making eye contact with the audience	Circle one: Yes / No Explain what you like or what could be improved about the students' speaking skills:
Visual and media displays are used to enhance the presentation	Circle one: Yes / No Explain what you like or what could be improved about the visual and media displays:

Teacher Resource F—Oral Presentation Peer-Assessment Form (*continued*)

Criteria	Your feedback
The students articulate one succinct, overarching opinion about the conflict	Circle one: Yes / No Write what the group's opinion is:
The students make at least 3 substantive points that draw from our class readings and support the overarching message	Circle one: Yes / No Summarize the 3 points:
The students share at least 2 next steps that they believe the government should take in reference to the conflict	Circle one: Yes / No Summarize the 2 next steps:

Next Steps: Third, review your feedback with the presenting group and ask the students to determine the next steps they will take to improve their work. Write the students' proposed next steps below.

1. _____

_____

2. _____

_____

3. _____

_____

Teacher Resource G—Sample Unit Timeline

Monday	Tuesday	Wednesday	Thursday	Friday
Community walk	Small-group and whole-class discussion—reflect on community walk and compose list of at least 10 community problems	Small-group and whole-class discussion—narrow list of 10 problems down to 2 or 3 that are most pressing	Independent reading—students choose 1 problem, of the 2 or 3 previously identified, and read teacher-selected articles on that problem	Prepare pre-sentations—students work in small groups to prepare short presenta-tions on the problem they studied
Student presentations	Open forum—choose 1 central problem for the civic literacy project	Mini-lesson on conducting research on the internet; independent internet-based research—study the efforts of organizations and agencies focused on problem	Independent internet-based research—study the efforts of organizations and agencies focused on problem	Open forum—determine if students will join a pre-existing campaign or initiative
Read poetry and/or narratives that document how individuals experience problem; independently annotate texts	Read poetry and/or narratives that document how individuals experience problem; independently annotate texts	Watch film that documents how individuals experience problem; small groups create and present posters on how individuals experience the problem	Prepare for community interviews where students will gather information on how community members experience problem	Rehearsal interviews with classmates

Teacher Resource G—Sample Unit Timeline (*continued*)

Monday	Tuesday	Wednesday	Thursday	Friday
Whole-class share-out— students share key information gathered during interviews	Small-group discussions— given the previous week of research, students determine what they want to say about their problem (i.e., they determine their message)	Deliberative forum— deliberate on 2–3 possible actions and choose action step (e.g., digital film PSA, persuasive letter, mural)	Study model action steps in the form the students chose (e.g., model PSAs)	Brainstorm and draft text for action step integrating elements from model texts
Continue drafting text	Peer review; submit text to teacher for teacher review	Review from a community member	Revise and edit text according to feedback from peers, teacher, and community member; small-group workshops or mini-lessons to address areas of need	Revise and edit text according to feedback from peers, teachers, and community member; small-group workshops or mini-lessons to address areas of need (add multiple days as necessary)
Distribute texts/execute action (add multiple days as necessary)	Reflect on action in small-group discussions and as a whole class	Whole-class brainstorming to propose next steps for the class or for other citizens working on related campaigns	Reflect on action and next steps in writing; share excerpts of writing	

Some activities might be recurring, as students are given opportunities to pursue particular skills over a course of days. This is the case during the second week of the unit outlined in Teacher Resource G when students engage in two consecutive days of research using the Internet. Or, a civic literacy project might entail a series of lessons in which students are working in small-group literature circles, with each circle reading about a different change maker who advocated for social justice. See, for example, the "defenders," presented in *Speak Truth to Power* (Kennedy, 2000), who have courageously advocated on a range of human rights issues. Each literature circle could read a piece about a different defender and his or her cause, one of which they will ultimately choose to put at the heart of their own class-wide project, and answer preprepared questions about that individual. To signify this period of time on a unit timeline, the teacher could repetitively write, "Meet in 'defender' literature circles; record responses to focus questions in journal" over a period of 3 days. This would signify that the performance task at hand is the completion of a literature circle journal, with either each group working with one journal or with each student completing his or her own journal. The key point is that timelines will sometimes illustrate that a singular activity will be ongoing over a series of days.

At other points in the unit, each day brings a unique task linked to a particular performance. For example, when students compose writing pieces (e.g., editorials or personal narratives on their experiences with a social problem), they might first outline their key ideas, then draft their pieces, and eventually revise based on peer, teacher, and self-assessment. These steps are unique, each occupying a day or multiple days on the timeline, yet they should be well connected, meaning that the sequencing should be logical.

Whether reinforcing particular skills through a recurring activity or learning a series of different but connected skills, timelines illustrate the amount of time and the sequenced instruction that the teacher will enact to support students to pursue their performance tasks. Ideally, the timelines will show that students will receive ample time and careful scaffolding so as to ensure their success. For example, if the guided inquiry performance asks the students to locate and reference outside sources, time should be allotted for this research, and teachers should teach mini-lessons on how to evaluate a found source to determine whether it will be helpful. If the culminating performance task is the creation of persuasive texts to be delivered to authentic audiences, students will benefit from a series of days, if not weeks, to create impacting work. On-demand writing, or stand-alone tasks, where students start and finish the piece within one sitting, can have particular limited value. Indeed, such tasks replicate the kinds of tasks students will complete on standardized tests. Yet, authentic learning is learning that is allowed to grow over time. And if students are to truly hone their activist voices through the civic literacy projects, they must be given time to allow these voices to emerge and sharpen.

Finally, timelines can indicate how the teacher will craft the unit around the students' emerging insights. For example, in Teacher Resource G—the sample timeline—one day within the second week is labeled accordingly: "Open forum—choose one central problem for the civic literacy project." On this day, the students will determine what social problem they wish to put at the heart of their project. Then, given whatever they choose, subsequent days in the timeline will be tailored or altered accordingly. Thus, when crafting a timeline, teachers propose estimations of how the unit will unfold while remaining attentive to the different ways their original, generalized visions will become more defined. Teachers can even consult with the students about drafts of the timeline or speak with the students about what they hope to happen in the project and intentionally fold their language into the timeline.

Drafting Lesson Plans

From the timeline level, the planning of day-to-day lessons begins. Here, teachers take the short descriptions of the lessons written on the timeline and transform them into detailed plans of how the lessons will be enacted. At this moment, they are thinking less about the entire scope of the unit as spanning over a month or so and more about how one period of instruction, perhaps lasting 45 or 90 minutes, will unfold. Yet, the long-term objectives and performance tasks should never be far away from their mind, as well-conceived lessons aid students in meeting the objectives and composing effective performances.

Lesson templates vary in format, with each one offering a different set of prompts. I believe the most essential prompts include lesson objective, lesson procedure, and forms of assessment. The lesson objective is a statement that begins with "Students will be able to . . . ," and then follows with a measurable verb such as "list," "describe," "compare," "debate," "write," or "present." These verbs are measurable because you can see, or observe, when someone is doing these things. In contrast, it is hard to know when a student "knows" or has "learned" something, and, therefore, these are not measurable verbs. They should be avoided in lesson objectives. The length of a lesson is so short that it is important for teachers to know exactly what they hope for students to get out of it. Establishing a measurable, or observable, objective helps with this. Some objectives that are particularly appropriate for civic literacy projects begin with the following:

- The students will be able to identify pressing social problems (in their community/in the world/etc.).
- The students will be able to evaluate multiple perspectives (concerning a particular social problem).
- The students will be able to critique sample (public service announcements/persuasive letters/etc.).
- The students will be able to brainstorm ideas (for their action steps).
- The students will be able to compose (personal narratives/persuasive texts/websites/etc.).

Next comes the lesson procedure, at the heart of the lesson. This is where teachers write the step-by-step moves the teacher and the students will take so that they can reach the lesson objective. This is the longest part of the lesson plan and is where teachers give themselves instructions to follow during the period. For example, if the lesson is describing an in-class deliberation on the topic of U.S. involvement in an international conflict (e.g., the civil war in Syria), three opening steps of the procedure might be as follows:

- Ask students to take out their issue maps summarizing four different stances on the U.S. Response to Syria (see Choices Program, 2013, "Debating the U.S. Response to Syria").
- Post summary statements of the four stances on the board.
- Prompt students to write down the stance to which they are most leaning, at the start of the deliberation, in their journals.

Then, following the deliberation, the students will have an opportunity to explain how, or if, their opinions changed.

In the assessment section of the lesson plan, teachers write in a sentence or list the ways that they will assess student learning during the lesson. Their tool for assessment might be a completed graphic organizer, class notes, or brief statements the students write summarizing what occurred in a section of a book or film they studied that day. It is essential that teachers examine student work created during lessons so as to understand what the students are learning. Student work is used as a means of conducting ongoing assessment in regard to the long-term objectives and performance tasks. For example, if students are working towards the creation of a website, their work during any one lesson can be assessed when the teacher views how the students are building knowledge of the content to be posted on the website, crafting language that articulates a clear message, and navigating web-based tools to launch the site.

Finally, sound lesson plans illustrate how teachers will aim to reach students with differing levels of ability. For example, teachers can plan to conduct a short mini-lesson with struggling students where they focus on a specific skill needed to accomplish a certain task. Or they can pair such students with more able students to work on a complex task that they could not accomplish alone. In these mixed-ability groups, students can assume roles that match their levels of ability while working on a shared task (Peterson, Hittie, & Tamor, 2002). Strategies for multilevel teaching can be marked throughout the procedure, or teachers can list particular differentiation strategies in a separate section of the lesson plan. However they are recorded, in order for all students to be involved in the civic literacy projects, teachers create targeted supports for students of all abilities.

CONCLUSION

Students' civic knowledge and skills are not developed spontaneously or through short-term exposures to political issues. Instead, in order for students to be involved in meaningful civic conversations and action, teachers bring to bear many existing theories about long-term performance-based curriculum design (e.g., Blythe & Associates, 1998; Jacobs, 1997; Wiggins & McTighe, 2005) when thinking through the enactment of civic literacy projects. This chapter illustrates how this can happen, proving the possible relationship between curriculum making and civic engagement. The phases presented throughout this book—problem identification, problem exploration, and action—are productively supported through a carefully crafted unit that is based around thought-provoking essential questions, authentic performances, and well-connected lessons. When civic curricula are designed in this way, civic literacy projects can become a part of the core curriculum—an essential step in preserving democracy.

References

Adler, M. J. (1982). *The Paideia proposal: An educational manifesto*. New York, NY: Touchstone.

Alexander, M. (2010). *The new Jim Crow: Mass incarceration in the age of color-blindness*. New York, NY: The New Press.

Alinsky, S. (1971). *Rules for radicals: A practice primer for realistic radicals*. New York, NY: Random House.

Anderson, L. H. (1999). *Speak*. New York, NY: Farrar, Straus and Giroux.

Apple, M. W. (2000). *Official knowledge: Democratic education in a conservative age*. New York, NY: Routledge.

Atwell, N. (1998). *In the middle: New understandings about writing, reading, and learning*. Portsmouth, NH: Heinemann.

Ayers, R., & Ayers, W. (2011). *Teaching the taboo: Courage and imagination in the classroom*. New York, NY: Teachers College Press.

Banks, J. A. (1993). The canon debate, knowledge construction, multicultural education. *Educational Researcher, 22*(5), 4–14.

Barber, B. (1992). *An aristocracy of everyone: The politics of education and the future of America*. New York, NY: Ballantine Books.

Barber, B. (2003). *Strong democracy: Participatory politics for a new age*. Berkeley, CA: University of California Press.

Barton, K. C., & Levstik, L. S. (1998). "It wasn't a good part of history": National identity and students' explanations of historical significance. *Teachers College Record, 99*(3), 478–513.

Beach, R., Thein, A. H., & Webb, A. (2012). *Teaching to exceed the English Language Arts Common Core State Standards: A literacy practices approach for 6–12 classrooms*. New York, NY: Routledge.

Bell, L. A. (2010). *Storytelling for social justice: Connecting narrative and the arts in antiracist teaching*. New York, NY: Routledge.

Berman, S. (2004). NCLB supplants our greatest teaching task since 9/11. *The Education Digest, 70*(2), 8–14.

Biesta, G. (2007). Education and the democratic person: Towards a political conception of democratic education. *Teachers College Record, 109*(3), 740–769.

Bigelow, B., Christensen, L., Karp, S., Miner, B., & Peterson, B. (1994). *Rethinking our classrooms: Teaching for equity and justice*. Milwaukee, MI: Rethinking Schools.

Bigelow, B., Harvey, B., Karp, S., & Miller, L. (2001). *Rethinking our classrooms: Teaching for equity and justice* (Vol. 2). Williston, VT: Rethinking Schools.

Billig, S. H., Jesse, D., Brodersen, R. M., & Grimley, M. (2008). Promoting secondary students' character development in schools through service-learning. In M. A. Bowdon, S. H. Billig, & B. A. Holland (Eds.), *Scholarship for sustaining service-learning and civic engagement* (pp. 57–83). Charlotte, NC: Information Age.

Blackburn, M. (2012). *Interrupting hate: Homophobia in schools and what literacy can do about it*. New York, NY: Teachers College Press.

Blythe, T., & Associates. (1998). *The teaching for understanding guide*. San Francisco, CA: Jossey-Bass.

Boal, A. (1979). *Theatre of the Oppressed*. New York, NY: Theatre Communications Group.

Bobbitt, F. (2009). Scientific method in curriculum-making. In D. J. Flinders & S. J. Thornton (Eds.), *The curriculum studies reader* (pp. 15–21). New York, NY: Routledge. (Original work published 1918)

Bomer, R. (2004). Speaking out for social action. *Education Leadership, 62*(2), 34–37.

Bomer, R., & Bomer, K. (2001). *For a better world: Reading and writing for social action*. Portsmouth, NH: Heinemann.

Brodsky, C. (1996). Ballad of Eddie Klepp. On *Letters in the dirt*. St. Paul, MN: Red House Records.

Choices Program. (2013). "Debating the U.S. response to Syria." Available at www.choices.edu/resources/twtn/twtn-syria-fall-2013.php

Christensen, L. (2000). *Reading, writing, and rising up: Teaching about social justice and the power of the written word*. Milwaukee, WI: Rethinking Schools.

Christensen, L. (2009). *Teaching for joy and justice: Re-imagining the language arts classroom*. Milwaukee, WI: Rethinking Schools.

Cipolle, S. B. (2010). *Service-learning and social justice: Engaging students in social change*. Lanham, MA: Rowman & Littlefield.

Cochran-Smith, M., & Lytle, S. L. (2006). Troubling images of teaching in No Child Left Behind. *Harvard Educational Review, 73*(4), 668–697.

Collins, P. H. (2010). The new politics of community. *American Sociological Review, 75*(1), 7–30.

Counts, G. S. (1932). *Dare the school build a new social order?* New York, NY: John Day.

Daniels, H., Zemelman, S., & Steineke, N. (2007). *Content-area writing: Every teacher's guide*. Portsmouth, NH: Heinemann.

Darts, D. (2006). Art education for a change: Contemporary issues and the visual arts. *Art Education, 59*(5), 6–12.

Dewey, J. (1897). *My pedagogic creed* (Vol. 18). New York, NY: E. L. Kellogg & Co.

Duffy, P. B. (2006). "I didn't know I had anything to say about racism": A personal account of Theatre of the Oppressed and high school students. *Stage of the Art, 17*(3), 5–6.

Duncan-Andrade, J. (2006). Urban youth, media literacy, and increased critical civic participation. In S. Ginwright, P. Noguera, & J. Cammarota (Eds.), *Beyond resistance! Youth activism and community change* (pp. 149–169). New York, NY: Routledge.

Eisner, E. W. (1985). *The educational imagination.* New York, NY: Macmillan.

Epstein, S. E. (2010). Activists and writers: Student expression in a social action literacy project. *Language Arts, 87*(5), 363–372.

Epstein, S. E., & Lipschultz, J. (2012). Getting personal? Student talk about racism. *Race Ethnicity and Education, 15*(3), 379–404.

Epstein, S. E., & Oyler, C. (2008). "An inescapable network of mutuality": Building relationships of solidarity in a first grade classroom. *Equity and Excellence in Education, 41*(4), 405–416.

Erentaite, R., Zukauskiene, R., Beyers, W., & Pilkauskaite-Valickiene, R. (2012). Is news media related to civic engagement? The effects of interest in and discussions about the news media on current and future civic engagement of adolescents. *Journal of Adolescence, 35*(3), 587–597.

Europa, D. (2013, August 1). With health care reform looming, clinics and patients brace for overcrowding. *South Kern Sol.* Available at www.southkernsol.org/2013/08/01/with-health-care-reform-looming-clinics-and-patients-brace-for-overcrowding

Evans, R. W. (2007). *This happened in America: Harold Rugg and the censure of social studies.* Charlotte, NC: Information Age.

Evans, R. W., Avery, P. G., & Pederson, P. V. (2000). Taboo topics: Cultural restraint on teaching social issues. *The Clearing House: A Journal of Educational Research, Controversy, and Practices, 73*(5), 295–302.

Fehrman, D., & Schutz, A. (2011). Beyond the Catch-22 of school-based social action programs: Toward a more pragmatic approach for dealing with power. *Democracy and Education, 19*(1), 1–9.

Feiman-Nemser, S. (1990). Teacher preparation: Structural and conceptual alternatives. In M. Haberman & J. Sikula (Eds.), *Handbook of research on teacher education* (pp. 212–233). New York, NY: Macmillan.

Felton, M. K., & Herko, S. (2004). From dialogue to two-sided argument: Scaffolding adolescents' persuasive writing. *Journal of Adolescent and Adult Literacy, 47*(8), 672–683.

Fisher, M. T. (2005). From the coffee house to the school house: The promise and potential of spoken word poetry in school contexts. *English Education, 37*(2), 115–131.

Flacks, M. (2007). "Label jars not people": How (not) to study youth civic engagement. In A. Best (Ed.), *Representing youth: Methodological issues in critical youth studies* (pp. 60–83). New York, NY: New York University Press.

Fletcher, R. (2010). Tips for young writers. Available at www.ralphfletcher.com/tips.html

Fletcher, S. (2000). *Education and emancipation: Theory and practice in a new constellation.* New York, NY: Teachers College Press.

Flores-Gonzalez, N., Rodriguez, M., & Rodriguez-Muniz, M. (2006). From hip-hop to humanization: Batey Urbano as a space for Latino youth culture and community action. In S. Ginwright, P. Noguera, & J. Cammarota (Eds.), *Beyond resistance! Youth activism and community change.* New York, NY: Routledge.

Freire, P. (1970). *Pedagogy of the oppressed.* New York, NY: Continuum.

Freire, P. (1973). *Education for critical consciousness.* New York, NY: Continuum.

Freire, P. (1985). *The politics of education: Culture, power and liberation.* Westport, CT: Bergin and Garvey.

Gaudelli, W., & Fernekes, W. R. (2004). Teaching about global human rights for global citizenship: Action research in the social studies curriculum. *The Social Studies, 95*(1), 16–26.

Gimpel, J. G., & Lay, J. C. (2006). Youth at-risk for non-participation. In P. Levine & J. Youniss (Eds.), *Youth civic engagement: An institutional turn* (pp. 10–15). College Park, MD: The Center for Information and Research on Civic Learning and Engagement. Available at www.civicyouth.org/PopUps/WorkingPapers/WP45LevineYouniss.pdf

Ginwright, S., & Cammarota, J. (2007). Youth activism in the urban community: Learning critical civic praxis within community organizations. *International Journal of Qualitative Studies in Education, 20*(6), 693–710.

Grazer, B. (Producer), & Howard, R. (Director). (2001). *A beautiful mind* [Motion picture]. U.S.: Universal Pictures.

Greene, M. (1995). *Releasing the imagination: Essays on education, the arts, and social change.* San Francisco, CA: Jossey-Bass.

Hallman, H. L. (2009). "Dear Tupac, you speak to me": Recruiting hip hop as curriculum at a school for pregnant and parenting teens. *Equity and Excellence in Education, 42*(1), 36–51.

Hart, S. (2009). The "problem" with youth: Young people, citizenship, and the community. *Citizenship Studies, 13*(6), 641–657.

Henderson, J. G., & Gornik, R. (2007). *Transformative curriculum leadership* (3rd ed.). Upper Saddle River, NJ: Pearson Merrill/Prentice Hall.

Hess, D. (2004). Beyond guest speakers. *Social Education, 68*(5), 347–348.

Hess, D. (2005). How do teachers' political views influence teaching about controversial issues? *Social Education, 69*(1), 47–48.

Hess, D. (2007). Teaching about global warming (Letter). *Social Education, 71*(7).

Hess, D. (2009a). *Controversy in the classroom: The democratic power of discussion.* New York, NY: Routledge.

Hess, D. (2009b). Principles that promote discussion of controversial political issues in the curriculum. In J. Youniss & P. Levine (Eds.), *Engaging young people in civic life* (pp. 59–77). Nashville, TN: Vanderbilt University Press.

Hess, D., & Marri, A. (2002). Which cases should we teach. *Social Education, 66*(1), 53–59.

Hirsch, E. D. (1996). *The schools we need: And why we don't have them.* New York, NY: Doubleday.

Howard, T. C. (2004). Social studies during the civil rights movement, 1955–1975. In C. Woyshner, J. Watras, & M. S. Crocco (Eds.), *Social education in the twentieth century: Curriculum and context for citizenship* (pp. 127–141). New York, NY: Peter Lang.

Hughes, L. (1994). Merry-go-round. In A. Rampersad & D. Roessel (Eds.), *The collected poems of Langston Hughes* (p. 240). New York, NY: Vintage Books.

Isaac, K. (1992). *Civics for democracy: A journey for teachers and students.* Washington, DC: Center for the Study of Responsive Law.

Jacobs, H. H. (1997). *Mapping the big picture: Integrating curriculum and assessment K–12.* Alexandria, VA: Association for Supervision and Curriculum Development.

Jansen, B. A. (2011). Civic education and the learning behaviors of youth in the online environment: A call for reform. *Journal of Social Studies Education Research, 2*(2), 22–42.

Jocson, K. M. (2006). "The best of both worlds": Youth poetry as social critique and form of empowerment. In S. Ginwright, P. A. Noguera, & J. Cammarota (Eds.), *Beyond resistance! Youth activism and community change* (pp. 129–147). New York, NY: Routledge.

Kahne, J., & Westheimer, J. (2006). The limits of efficacy: Educating citizens for a democratic society. *PS–Political Science and Politics, 39*(2), 289–296.

Kelly, D. M. (2006). Frame work: Helping youth counter their misrepresentations in media. *Canadian Journal of Education, 29*(1), 27–48.

Kennedy, K. (2000). *Speak truth to power.* Brooklyn, NY: Umbrage Editions.

Kesson, K., & Oyler, C. (1999). Integrated curriculum and service-learning: Linking school-based knowledge and social action. *English Education, 31*(2), 135–149.

Kincheloe, J., & McLaren, P. (2003). Rethinking critical theory and qualitative research. In N. K. Denzin & Y. S. Lincoln (Eds.), *The landscape of qualitative research: Theories and issues* (2nd ed., pp. 433–488). Thousand Oaks, CA: Sage.

Kirshner, B. (2006). Apprenticeship learning in youth activism. In S. Ginwright, P. Noguera, & J. Cammarota (Eds.), *Beyond resistance: Youth activism and community change* (pp. 37–57). New York, NY: Routledge.

Kirshner, B. (2009). "Power in numbers": Youth organizing as a context for exploring civic identity. *Journal of Research on Adolescents, 19*(3), 414–440.

Kleyn, T. (2011). *Immigration: The ultimate teen guide.* Lanham, MD: Scarecrow Press.

Kliebard, H. M. (1995). *The struggle for the American curriculum* (2nd ed.). New York, NY: Routledge.

Kozol, J. (1996). *Amazing grace: The lives of children and the conscience of a nation.* New York, NY: Harper Perennial.

Kubey, R. (2004). Media literacy and the teaching of civics and social studies at the dawn of the 21st century. *American Behavioral Scientist, 48*(1), 69–77.

Kurusa. (1981). *The streets are free.* Toronto, ON: Annick Press.

Kwon, S. A. (2008). Moving from complaints to action: Oppositional consciousness and collective action in a political community. *Anthropology & Education Quarterly, 39*(1), 59–76.

Laviano, M. (2007). Teaching about global warming (Letter). *Social Education, 71*(7).

Lee, H. (1960). *To kill a mockingbird.* Philadelphia, PA: HarperCollins.

Lensmire, T. J. (1998). Rewriting student voice. *Journal of Curriculum Studies, 30*(3), 261–291.

Lester, B. T., Ma, L., Lee, O., & Lambert, J. (2006). Social activism in elementary science education: A science, technology, and society approach to teach global warming. *International Journal of Science Education, 28*(4), 315–339.

Leu, D. J. (1997). Caity's question: Literacy as deixis on the Internet. *The Reading Teacher, 51*(1), 62–67.

Levine, P. (2007). *The future of democracy: Developing the next generation of American citizens.* Medford, MA: Tufts University Press.

Levine, P. (2011). Letter to President Obama: A policy approach for the federal government. In D. Feith (Ed.), *Teaching America: The case for civic education* (pp. 209–217). Lanham, MA: Rowman & Littlefield.

Levine, P. (2013). *We are the ones we have been waiting for: The promise of civic renewal in America.* New York, NY: Oxford University Press.

Levinson, B. (2005). Citizenship, identity, democracy: Engaging the political in the anthropology of education. *Anthropology & Education Quarterly, 36*(4), 329–340.

Lewis-Charp, H., Yu, H. C., & Soukamneuth, S. (2006). Civic activist approaches for engaging youth in social justice. In S. Ginwright, P. Noguera, & J. Cammarota (Eds.), *Beyond resistance: Youth activism and community change* (pp. 21–53). New York, NY: Routledge.

Lipman, P. (2007). *High stakes education: Inequality, globalization, and urban school reform.* New York, NY: RoutledgeFalmer.

Loewen, J. W. (2007). *Lies my teacher told me: Everything your American history textbook got wrong.* New York, NY: Simon & Schuster.

London, S. (2013). *Immigration in America: How do we fix a system in crisis?* Dayton, OH: National Issues Forums Institute.

Lopez, M. H., Levine, P., Dautrich, K., & Yalof, D. (2009). Schools, education policy, and the future of the First Amendment. *Political Communication, 26,* 84–101.

Makler, A. (2004). "Problems of democracy" and the social studies curriculum during the long armistice. In C. Woyshner, J. Watras, & M. S. Crocco (Eds.), *Social education in the twentieth century* (pp. 20–41). New York, NY: Peter Lang.

Marri, A. R., Ahn, M., Crocco, M. S., Grolnick, M., Gaudelli, W., & Walker, E. N. (2012). Teaching the federal budget, national debt, and budget deficit: Findings from high school teachers. *The Social Studies, 102*(5), 204–210.

Maxwell, Z. (2012). *Yuck—A 4th grader's short documentary about school lunch.* Available at www.yuckmovie.com

Mayo, J. B. J. (2013). Critical pedagogy enacted in the gay–straight alliance: New possibilities for a third space in teacher development. *Educational Researcher, 42*(5), 266–275.

McLaughlin, M., & DeVoogd, G. (2004). Critical literacy as comprehension: Expanding reader response. *Journal of Adolescent and Adult Literacy, 48*(1), 52–62.

Melber, L. M., & Hunter, A. (2010). *Integrating language arts and social studies.* Thousand Oaks, CA: Sage.

Miller, A. (2003). *The crucible.* New York, NY: Penguin.

Moje, E. B., Dillon, D. R., & O'Brien, D. (2000). Reexamining roles of learner, text, and context in secondary literacy. *The Journal of Educational Research, 93*(3), 165–180.

Moje, E. B., Overby, M., Tysvaer, N., & Morris, K. (2008). The complex world of adolescent literacy: Myths, motivations, and mysteries. *Harvard Educational Review, 78*(1), 107–154.

Moll, L. C., Amanti, C., Neff, D., & Gonzalez, N. (1992). Funds of knowledge for teaching: Using a qualitative approach to connect homes and classrooms. *Theory into Practice, 31*(2), 132–141.

Morrell, E., Duenas, R., Garcia, V., & Lopez, J. (2013). *Critical media pedagogy: Teaching for achievement in city schools.* New York, NY: Teachers College Press.

Mullen, A. (2004). "Some sort of revolution": Reforming the social studies curriculum, 1957–1972. In C. Woyshner, J. Watras, & M. S. Crocco (Eds.), *Social education in the twentieth century* (pp. 110–126). New York, NY: Peter Lang.

Myers, J. P., & Zaman, H. A. (2009). Negotiating the global and national: Immigrant and dominant-culture adolescents' vocabularies of citizenship in a transnational world. *Teachers College Record, 111*(11), 2589–2625.

National Council for the Social Studies (1971). *Social studies curriculum guidelines.* Washington, DC: Author.

National Council for the Social Studies. (2002). *National standards for social studies teachers.* Available at downloads.ncss.org/NCSSTeacherStandardsVol1-rev 2004.pdf

National Council of Teachers of English & the International Reading Association. (2009). *Standards for the English language arts.* Available at www.ncte.org/standards

National Governors Association Center for Best Practices, Council of Chief State School Officers. (2010). *Common Core State Standards.* Washington, DC: Author.

National Issues Forums Institute. (2013). *How can we stop mass shootings in our communities?* Dayton, OH: Author. Available at www.nifi.org/issue_books/detail.aspx?catID=6&itemID=23757

Nieto, S. (1994). Affirmation, solidarity and critique: Moving beyond tolerance in education. *Multicultural Magazine, 1*(4), 9–12.

Noguera, P. A. (2003). *City schools and the American dream: Reclaiming the promise of public education.* New York, NY: Teachers College Press.

Oakes, J., & Rogers, J. (2006). *Learning power: Organizing for education and justice.* New York, NY: Teachers College Press.

Ogden, C. (1999). Going beyond service. In J. Claus & C. Ogden (Eds.), *Service-learning for youth empowerment and social change* (pp. 187–192). New York, NY: Peter Lang.

Oyler, C. (1996). *Making room for students: Sharing authority in Room 104.* New York, NY: Teachers College Press.

Oyler, C. (2012). *Actions speak louder than words: Community activism as curriculum.* New York, NY: Routledge.

Pak, Y. K. (2004). Teaching for intercultural understanding in the social studies: A teacher's perspective in the 1940s. In C. Woyshner, J. Watras, & M. S. Crocco (Eds.), *Social education in the twentieth century* (pp. 57–75). New York, NY: Peter Lang.

Parker, W. C. (1997). Navigating the unity/diversity tension in education for democracy. *The Social Studies, 88*(1), 12–17.

Parker, W. C. (2003). *Teaching democracy: Unity and diversity in public life.* New York, NY: Teachers College Press.

Peck, A. (2013). Ban the box! A role play on mass incarceration. *Rethinking Schools, 27*(4), 52–57.

Peterson, M., Hittie, M., & Tamor, L. (2002). *Authentic, multi-level teaching: Teaching children with diverse academic abilities together well.* Detroit, MI: Wayne State University, Whole Schooling Consortium.

Powell, R., Cantrell, S. C., & Adams, S. (2001). Saving Black Mountain: The promise of critical literacy in a multicultural democracy. *The Reading Teacher, 54*(8), 772–781.

Rivera, T. (2007). *And the earth did not devour him.* New York, NY: Hampton Brown.

Robinson, J. (1998). Literacy and lived lives: Reflections on the responsibilities of teachers. In C. Fleischer & D. Schaafsma (Eds.), *Literacy and democracy: Teacher research and composition studies in pursuit of habitable spaces* (pp. 1–27). Urbana, IL: National Council of Teachers of English.

Rogovin, P. (1998). *Classroom interviews: A world of learning.* Portsmouth, NH: Heinemann.

Rubin, B. C. (2007). "There's still not justice": Youth civic identity development amid distinct school and community contexts. *Teachers College Record, 109*(2), 449–481.

Rubin, B. C., & Hayes, B. F. (2010). "No backpacks" versus "drugs and murder": The promise and complexity of youth civic action research. *Harvard Educational Review, 80*(30), 352–379.

Rubin, B. C., Hayes, B. F., & Benson, K. (2009). "It's the worst place to live": Urban youth and the challenge of school-based civic learning. *Theory into Practice, 48*(3), 213–221.

Russell, W. B. (2009). *Teaching social issues with film.* Scottsdale, AZ: Information Age.

Schlosser, E. (2001). *Fast food nation: The dark side of the all-American meal.* New York, NY: First Mariner Books.

Schoenbach, R., Greenleaf, C., Cziko, C., & Hurwitz, L. (1999). *Reading for understanding: A guide to improving reading in middle and high school classrooms.* San Francisco, CA: Jossey-Bass.

Schultz, B. D. (2008). *Spectacular things happen along the way: Lessons from an urban classroom.* New York, NY: Teacher College Press.

Schultz, K. (2009). *Rethinking classroom participation: Listening to student voices.* New York, NY: Teachers College Press.

Schutz, A. (2006). Home is a prison in the global city: The tragic failure of school-based community engagement strategies. *Review of Educational Research, 76*(4), 691–743.

Seixas, P. (1994). Students' understanding of historical significance. *Theory and Research in Social Education, 22*(3), 281–304.

Sen, I. (2013, May 10). The Michael Moore of the grade-school lunchroom. *The New York Times*, p. A24.

Shakespeare, W. (1992). *The taming of the shrew*. New York, NY: Washington Square Press.

Shakur, A. (1987). *Assata: An autobiography*. Chicago, IL: Lawrence Hill.

Simon, L., & Norton, N. E. L. (2011). A mighty river: Intersections of spiritualities and activism in children's and young adult literature. *Curriculum Inquiry, 41*(2), 293–318.

Sinclair, U. (2001). *The jungle*. Mineola, NY: Dover. (Original work published 1906)

Speak truth to power: Human rights defenders who are changing our world. (2010). Washington, DC: Robert F. Kennedy Center for Justice and Human Rights and New York States United Teachers (NYSUT). Available at locals.nysut.org /speaktruth_curriculum_complete.pdf

Spring, J. (1989). *The sorting machine revisited: National educational policy since 1945*. New York, NY: Longman.

Steinbeck, J. (1939). *The grapes of wrath*. New York, NY: Penguin.

Steinbeck, J. (1982). *Of mice and men*. New York, NY: Bantam.

Sutherland-Smith, W. (2002). Weaving the literacy web: Changes in reading from page to screen. *The Reading Teacher, 55*(7), 662–669.

Takaki, R. (1993). *A different mirror: A history of multicultural America*. New York, NY: Back Bay Books.

Teacher's guide to National Issues Forums (NIF) in the classroom. (2001). Dayton, OH: National Issues Forums Institute.

Torney-Purta, J., Barber, C. H., & Richardson, W. K. (2005). How teachers' preparation relates to students' civic knowledge and engagement in the United States: Analysis from the IEA Civic Education Study. College Park, MD: The Center for Information and Research on Civic Learning and Engagement.

Torney-Purta, J., Barber, C. H., & Wilkenfeld, B. (2007). Latino adolescents' civic development in the United States: Research results from the IEA Civic Education Study. *Journal of Youth Adolescence, 36*, 111–125.

Tyack, D., & Cuban, L. (1995). *Tinkering toward utopia: A century of public school reform*. Cambridge, MA: Harvard University Press.

Understanding fiscal responsibility (UFR): A curriculum for teaching about the federal budget, national debt, and budget deficit. (2012). Available at teachufr.org /about

VanSledright, B. (2002). *In search of America's past: Learning to read history in elementary school*. New York, NY: Teachers College Press.

Wade, R. (1997). Community service-learning and the social studies curriculum: Challenges to effective practice. *The Social Studies, 88*, 197–202.

Wade, R. (2000). From a distance: Service-learning and social justice. In C. O'Grady (Ed.), *Integrating service-learning and multicultural education in colleges and universities* (pp. 93–112). Mahwah, NJ: Lawrence Erlbaum Associates.

Wade, R. (2001). Social action in the social studies: From the ideal to the real. *Theory into Practice, 40*(1), 23–28.

Warren, M. R. (2001). *Dry bones rattling: Community building to revitalize American democracy.* Princeton, NJ: Princeton University Press.

Watras, J. (2004). Historians and social studies educators, 1893–1998. In C. Woyshner, J. Watras, & M. S. Crocco (Eds.), *Social education in the twentieth century* (pp. 192–209). New York, NY: Peter Lang.

Wei, D. (2006). Students' stories in action comics. In E. Lee, D. Menkart, & M. Okazawa-Rey (Eds.), *Beyond heroes and holidays: A practical guide to K–12 anti-racist, multicultural education and staff development* (pp. 216–225). Washington, DC: Teaching for Change.

Westheimer, J. (2007). Politics and patriotism in education. In J. Westheimer (Ed.), *Pledging allegiance: The politics of patriotism in America's schools* (pp. 171–188). New York, NY: Teachers College Press.

Westheimer, J., & Kahne, J. (2004). What kind of citizen?: The politics of educating for democracy. *American Educational Research Journal, 41*(2), 237–269.

Wiggins, G., & McTighe, J. (2005). *Understanding by design.* Alexandria, VA: Association for Supervision and Curriculum Development.

Wilhelm, J. D. (2007). *Engaging readers and writers with inquiry: Promoting deep understandings in language arts and the content areas with guiding questions.* New York, NY: Scholastic.

Wong, J. (1994). Waiting at the railroad cafe. In J. Wong (Ed.), *Good luck gold and other poems.* (p. 8). Princeton, NJ: Poetry Suitcase.

Young Women's Leadership School of Brooklyn. (2013). Modern slavery and sex trafficking. Available at www.speaktruthvideo.com

Youniss, J., McLellan, J. A., & Yates, M. (1997). What we know about engendering civic identity. *American Behavioral Scientist, 40*(5), 620–631.

Zinn, H. (2003). *A people's history of the United States.* New York, NY: HarperCollins.

Zinn, H., & Arnove, A. (2004). *Voices of a people's history of the United States.* New York, NY: Seven Stories Press.

Index

About the Author

Shira Eve Epstein, Ed.D., entered the field of education as a middle school teacher in New York City. She is now a professor at The City College of New York (CUNY) in the Department of Secondary Education. She teaches courses in teaching methods for secondary English language arts, curriculum design, and literacy development for graduate and undergraduate in-service and preservice teachers. In her research she explores different forms of civic education and how teachers and students address social problems through curriculum. Her writing analyzes the enacted pedagogy of civic projects, educators' perspectives and experiences during such projects, and students' responses. She also studies anti-racist education, pursuing various related lines of inquiry such as how youth talk about race. Her work can be found in scholarly publications including *Language Arts, The Journal of Social Studies Research, Journal of Teacher Education,* and *Race Ethnicity and Education.* She primarily learns from teachers and students in urban schools and after-school programs.